P9-DEX-956

ZECHARIAH'S PROPHETIC VISION FOR THE NEW WORLD

Virtually all Scripture references are quoted from the King James translation of the Holy Bible.

Zechariah's Prophetic Vision For The New World
Copyright © 2002, © 2007 by Midnight Call Ministries
West Columbia, South Carolina 29170
Published by The Olive Press, a division of Midnight Call Ministries
Columbia, SC 29228 U.S.A.

An Olive Press Production

  Copy Typist: Lynn Jeffcoat, Kathy Roland
  Copy Editor: Susanna Cancassi
  Proofreaders: Angie Peters, Susanna Cancassi
Layout/Design: Michelle Kim
  Lithography: Simon Froese
 Cover Design: Michelle Kim

Library of Congress Cataloging-in-Publication Data

Lieth, Norbert
   Zechariah's Prophetic Vision For The New World
   ISBN# 0-937422-56-8

   1. Prophecy

All rights reserved. No portion of this book may be reproduced in any form without the written permission of the publisher.

Printed in the United States of America

*This book is dedicated to the
Church of Jesus Christ worldwide.*

*It is intended to contribute toward a better
understanding of God's counsel to men
based on the Scripture.*

*The author does not benefit through
royalties from the proceeds
of the sale of this book. All received funds
are reinvested for the furtherance
of the Gospel.*

Translated from German by Ann Fankhauser
Der Prophet Sacharja: Vision für eine neue Zeit
Copyright © 2002 by Mitternachtsruf CH

FOREWORD

It was Midnight Call founder, Dr. Wim Malgo's heartfelt wish to write a book on the prophet Zechariah. He was not able to accomplish this task because he was called home to glory on August 8, 1992. Since then, I have had an inner desire to undertake this project myself. I am very grateful to God that He has given me the grace to complete this book.

At this point, I would like to express my deepest appreciation to my co-workers who encouraged me to write this book. And special thanks to all those who made the English translation of this book possible. Ann Fankhauser has diligently worked for many hours translating the manuscript into English. Susanna Cancassi and Angie Peters were responsible for the editorial and proofreading process, and Michelle Kim did a fine job on the cover design. Above all, thanks be to our Lord Jesus Christ who has answered our prayers and watched over this entire project from start to finish.

The entire biblical text is written at the beginning of each chapter so that the reader does not have to look each reference up in the Bible. Within each chapter, we have also quoted the individual verses again, so that the reader has the words before him. We have noted instances where we have used a translation other than the King James.

The exposition of the Old Testament book of Zechariah could certainly be developed much deeper than what I have presented here. But I want to emphasize that I wrote this book according to my own personal understanding of the Scriptures. Some people may see certain things differently, and they may be right; however, I hope and pray that this commentary encourages many to study the Scriptures for themselves.

The book of Zechariah wonderfully portrays our faithful and reliable God who will not let even one of His promises fail, and that we are being led toward the glory of Jesus Christ. The tribulation and confusion of our time are not the end, but the end will be marked by Jesus' return to set up His kingdom in which righteousness and peace will reign.

Norbert Lieth
Pfäffikon, Switzerland, October 2002

CONTENTS

INTRODUCTION

The Old Testament book of Zechariah was written around 520 B.C. Zechariah, whose name means "the Lord remembers," came from the tribe of Levi. He was a priest, born in Babylon (compare to Zechariah 1:1 and Nehemiah 12:1,4 & 6). Therefore, like Jeremiah and Ezekiel, Zechariah was a priest and prophet simultaneously.

Zechariah contains a tremendous revelation regarding the Name of God. The Name used most frequently, *"the Lord of hosts,"* occurs approximately 50 times. In fact, it appears 3 times in 1:3 alone: *"Therefore say thou unto them, thus saith the LORD of hosts; Turn ye unto me, saith the LORD of hosts, and I will turn unto you, saith the LORD of hosts."*

Zechariah wrote in great detail about various aspects of Israel.

• Israel's restoration is discussed 19 times (1:16–17, 2:12, 3:10, 8:7–8, 12–15, 19, 9:8,16, 10:3, 6–8 & 9–12, 12:4, 6–8,10, 13:9, 14:8, 10–11,16,20).

• Israel's future forgiveness is mentioned 7 times

(3:2–4,9, 5:8, 10:6,8, 13:1 and 14:11).

• Nine times it says that the Lord will dwell in the midst of His people (i.e. the Temple) (2:5,14,15, 6:13, 8:3,8,22–23, 9:8 and 14:9).

There are also other striking repetitions of terms:

• The words "nations," "peoples," and other related terms appear 24 times.

• The words *"Jerusalem," "Zion,"* and other references to Jerusalem ("city," for instance) appear 44 times.

• References to Jesus as the *"stone," "headstone"* or *"cornerstone"* appear 5 times (twice in 3:9, 4:7,10 and 10:4).

By finishing the Temple at that time, Zerubbabel serves as a hidden pointer to Jesus, the Author and Finisher of our faith (as in Haggai 2:23, *"In that day, saith the LORD of hosts, will I take thee, O Zerubbabel, my servant, the son of Sheattiel, saith the LORD and will make thee as a signet: for I have chosen thee saith the LORD of hosts."*)

• At least 12 times it is written that the Lord will reign over the entire world in the future, that He has His eye on all of the nations, and that He is their Judge (2:11–13, 4:10,14, 6:5,15, 8:22, 9:10, 12:2–4, 14:2–3, 9, 12, 16–19; compare also Acts 17:31 and Hebrews 2:5–8).

• Six times we read that Israel will know the Lord and will repent (2:9,11, 4:9, 6:15, 12:10–14 and 13:6).

• We read about the Lord's return 5 times (2:10, 8:3, 9:14, 12:10 and 14:5).

Together with Haggai and Malachi, Zechariah belongs to the three so-called "post-exile prophets" or "prophets of the return." He belonged to a group of 42,360 people (Ezra 2:64) who returned to Jerusalem from Babylonian captivity through the decree of Persia's King Cyrus (Ezra 1:2–4 and Isaiah 44:28). Ezra, Zerubbabel, Joshua, and Nehemiah also belonged to the number who returned.

Zechariah was a contemporary of the prophet Haggai (Ezra 5:1 and 6:14). He began his ministry as a prophet only two months after Haggai's first message (compare Haggai 1:1 and Zechariah 1:1). Yet, while Haggai rebuked and admonished the Jewish people in Jerusalem not to be negligent in rebuilding the Temple, Zechariah's message is more one of glad tidings regarding the future. The prophets presented two quite different, yet complementary, messages, and both were important and necessary for the people. Haggai only wrote 2 chapters; Zechariah wrote 14. Zechariah, like Jeremiah, was called to be a prophet as a very young man (Zechariah 2:4, also see Jeremiah 1:6–7). On the other hand, we understand that Haggai was probably older. While Haggai only prophesied for a few months, Zechariah's ministry probably lasted 30 or more years. Haggai proclaimed more practical application of God's Word. His message focused on the Israelites negligence in rebuilding the Temple. Zechariah spoke more about prophecy, dealing with Israel's future and her spiritual restoration. Regarding Israel's future, Zechariah says more in his 14 chapters than any other prophet. This, however, does not mean that Haggai's message was not prophetic; nor does it mean that Zechariah's message was without instruction or correction.

The book of Zechariah is described as the most Messianic, apocalyptic and eschatological of all Old Testament Scriptures; therefore, Zechariah is the most Christ-centered prophet of the Old Covenant. He speaks more about Christ, His work and glory than all of the other minor prophets combined. The Scofield Bible says that no prophetic book in the Old Testament contains so many prophecies concerning Christ, Israel and the nations, in such a short amount of space as Zechariah. Martin Luther described the book of Zechariah as the quintessence of the prophets.

With regard to the person of Christ, Zechariah writes about the Branch who will come as the crowned Priest and King. We also find a vision of Jesus' entry into Jerusalem on a donkey, which combines the First and Second Coming of Christ. We see Him as the One who was pierced on the Cross, the One who was smitten by the sword of God. We see Him as the true Shepherd, in contrast to the foolish shepherd, who is a picture of the Antichrist. Jesus is portrayed as the One who will return to the Mount of Olives for the salvation of His people. Zechariah's prophecies concern Jesus' First and Second Comings, including His future rule, His priesthood, His kingship, His humanity, His divinity, His building of the Temple, His coming in humility, His bringing of peace, His rejection and reacceptance, His betrayal for thirty pieces of silver and other things.

Further, in his general prophecies, Zechariah describes the last attack of Jerusalem by the nations, the initial victory of the enemies, the division of the Mount of Olives, the defense of Jerusalem through the Lord's return, His judgment upon the nations and the changing of the earth's surface in the land of Israel. He also describes the glory of the Lord that fills the Temple. He explains the Feast of Tabernacles in the millennium of peace, in which other nations will be joined to His people. And finally, He explains that living water will flow from the Temple in Jerusalem. He prophesies that all Israel's sins will be forgiven and speaks of the ultimate holiness of Jerusalem and the Jews.

Surely this is the reason there are over 40 quotations and references to Zechariah in the New Testament (compare Zechariah 12:10 and Revelation 1:7, for instance). Certainly this must be a reason that the Jewish rabbis do not know what to do with this book. For instance, Abrabanel, a great Jewish exegete and author of many commentaries, confessed that he was not capable of explaining Zechariah's visions. This is no wonder, considering that he denies that Jesus of Nazareth is the Messiah (compare to Acts 2:36). Solomon ben Yarchi, another exegete highly esteemed by the Jews, declared that Zechariah's prophecy is very hard to understand because it contains dream like visions, the interpretation of which is not available to us, so we shall never be able to find its true exegesis until the Teacher of Righteousness comes. From such statements we see that the Old Testament remains closed to all who do not possess the key — this key is the Lord Jesus Christ! For instance, the Ethiopian eunuch was unable to understand Isaiah 53 because he did not know Jesus (Acts 8:30–39).

Zechariah's message contains God's plans for Israel's future and relevant promises for the future salvation of the Jews. This is why Zechariah is also called "the great prophet of restoration."

Four men are named in Ezra 5:1–2 who played main roles in the rebuilding of the Temple: Zerubbabel, Haggai, Joshua and Zechariah. This is a picture of Jesus Christ as He is presented in the four Gospels in their prophetic portrayal.

Zerubbabel was the governor and ruler of Israel. He is an example of the Lord Jesus as He is portrayed in Matthew's Gospel account. He is God's anointed King, to whom the future power as ruler in Israel is given.

Haggai was a servant and prophet, and is therein a picture of the Lord in Mark's Gospel account: Jesus, the humble servant of God.

Joshua was the high priest. He presents Jesus as we see Him in Luke's Gospel account: The sinless Son of man, high priest and mediator between God and man.

Zechariah the prophet particularly emphasized Jesus' divinity. Therewith, he is a picture of Jesus as shown in John's Gospel account: Jesus, the Son of God, who came to this earth.

What can we learn from these sketches?

First, as New Testament kings and priests, we should be bearers of the revelation of Jesus' Name. He is the Savior of the world. In Acts 4:12, Peter said: *"Neither is there salvation in any other: for there is none other name under heaven given among men, whereby we must be saved"* (compare also to Acts 3:6,16, and 4:7,10,12,17,18).

Second, God, in His wisdom, places young and old beside one another in His service. In our age of the Church, no one is too old or too young to be called to follow and serve Jesus. Timothy was encouraged, *"Let no man despise thy youth"* (1st Timothy 4:12), and Psalm 148:12–13 reads: *"Both young men, and maidens; old men, and children: let them praise the name of the LORD: for his name alone is excellent; his glory is above the earth and heaven."* The Lord said to Jeremiah, *"Say not, I am a child."* (Jeremiah 1:7). If God speaks to your heart, then you are old enough!

Further, we learn that all diverse gifts and tasks come from the Giver of all gifts. Zechariah could have said to Haggai, "Why don't you preach a bit more on prophecy and the hope for the future?" And Haggai could have answered, "What about you? Why don't you stop thinking about the future all the time? The people need instruction, admonition and sanctification to build the Temple. Practical things are also necessary; we are living here and now!" But they did not quarrel. They both fulfilled their tasks faithfully and with endurance, just as God had commissioned them.

Recently I heard a preacher say that there is too much evangelization, and what we really need is more sanctification. But at the same time, in a different place, someone else said that the Church is far too concerned with herself and 75% of all sermons should be evangelistic! Regarding God's calling: *"And he gave some, apostles; and some, prophets; and some, evangelists; and some, pastors and teachers; for the perfecting of the saints, for the work of the ministry, for the edifying of the body of Christ"* (Ephesians 4:11–12).

The book of Zechariah also stresses the importance of a Christ-centered life and of a message and work, that point people to Him: *"For I determined not to know any thing among you, save Jesus Christ, and him crucified"* (1st Corinthians 2:2). We must be aware that without Jesus, the Bible is only a book with seven seals. This is especially true with regard to Israel. Only the Spirit of Jesus, the Spirit of truth, can guide us into all truth: *"When he, the Spirit of truth, is come, he will guide you into all truth: for he shall not speak of himself; but whatsoever he shall hear, that shall he speak: and he will shew you things to come. He shall glorify me: for he shall receive of mine, and shall shew it unto you"* (John 16:13–14).

Finally, we learn that we must not lose our vision of the future. The day is coming when Jesus will return and the light of His kingdom will surpass everything we have ever seen: *"And ye now therefore have sorrow: but I will see you again, and your heart shall rejoice, and your joy no man taketh from you"* (John 16:22).

CHAPTER 1

THREE CRUCIAL POINTS OF ENCOURAGEMENT

"In the eighth month, in the second year of Darius, came the word of the LORD unto Zechariah, the son of Berechiah, the son of Iddo the prophet, saying, The LORD hath been sore displeased with your fathers. Therefore say thou unto them, Thus saith the LORD of hosts; Turn ye unto me, saith the LORD of hosts, and I will turn unto you, saith the LORD of hosts. Be ye not as your fathers, unto whom the former prophets have cried, saying, Thus saith the LORD of hosts; Turn ye now from your evil ways, and from your evil doings: but they did not hear, nor hearken unto me, saith the LORD. Your fathers, where are they? and the prophets, do they live for ever? But my words and my statutes, which I commanded my servants the prophets, did they not take hold of your fathers? and they returned and said, Like as the LORD of hosts thought to do unto us, according to our ways, and according to our doings, so

hath he dealt with us" (Zechariah 1:1–6).

God led His people out of their 70-year Babylonian captivity and brought them back to Jerusalem, fulfilling the promise He made through Jeremiah the prophet (Jeremiah 25:11–12 and 29:10–14). The Lord was giving the Jews a completely new perspective: The possibility of rebuilding Jerusalem, particularly the Temple, and the wall around Jerusalem. They would live, sacrifice and serve God in their city again.

The Lord sent Zechariah the prophet and gave those returning home a new hope for the future. He showed them new possibilities, and above all, the glorious future that would be theirs under the Messiah's reign. Israel would receive a new vision and would recognize God's plan for its future. God wanted to encourage the Israelites through Zechariah to take advantage of the opportunity and to dedicate themselves wholly to Him. The new work was not to be delayed. Israel was to give the Lord first priority, and this is the theme of Zechariah's first six verses.

"Therefore say thou unto them, Thus saith the LORD of hosts; Turn ye unto me, saith the LORD of hosts, and I will turn unto you, saith the LORD of hosts" (verse 3). Complete dedication is always a condition for the success of a new task. The Old Testament book of Haggai explains how grave a delay can be: *"Ye looked for much, and, lo, it came to little; and when ye brought it home, I did blow upon it. Why?*

saith the LORD of hosts. Because of mine house that is waste, and ye run every man unto his own house" (Haggai 1:9).

Likewise, the Lord continually presents us with new possibilities because He wants to lead us from our confinement into the wide open spaces. He wants to ignite hope in us. A great work demands great faithfulness, dedication and zeal. The Lord introduces three crucial points to encourage His people to rededicate themselves:

1. Encouragement Through Three Names

"In the eighth month, in the second year of Darius, came the word of the LORD unto Zechariah, the son of Berechiah, the son of Iddo the prophet" (Zechariah 1:1). God presented King Darius of the Persians with three Hebrew names. Darius ruled over the known world, which included Israel, at that time. Although the Jews were granted permission to return to their homeland, they were still subject to Darius' authority.

The time of the nations began with Babylon under Nebuchadnezzar's leadership when he destroyed Jerusalem and led Judah into captivity (2nd Chronicles 36:10–21). The time of the nations continued over the Persian, Greek and Roman Empires, and will last until the Lord returns to judge the nations and begin His reign in Israel (Luke 21:24 and Revelation 16:19). The fact that a Gentile king ruled continually was a reminder to the Jews that, despite their return to their land, they remained under the rule of the nations.

The Bible also says that while believers are still *in* the world, we are no longer *of* this world (John 17:15–16). But it seems as though God wanted to use Zechariah's first sentence to remind His people that this would not always be the case; thus, their hope was grounded in God's promises. Similarly, our living hope is based not on the things of this earth, but on the future.

Three names are revealed in Zechariah 1:1:

*"...came the word of the LORD unto **Zechariah**, the son of **Berechiah**, the son of **Iddo**."* Let's take a look at what each means:

- *Zechariah* = Jehovah: "The Lord remembers"
- *Berechiah* = Blessed by Jehovah: "The Lord will bless"
- *Iddo* = "Born at an appointed time"

The name *Zechariah* draws our attention to the fact that the Lord will never forget the promises He made to the patriarchs: *"Can a woman forget her sucking child, that she should not have compassion on the son of my womb? yea, they may forget, yet will I not forget thee. Behold, I have graven thee upon the palms of my hands; thy walls are continually before me"* (Isaiah 49:15–16). God's promises are infallible. He never regrets any of them! Even if the Gentiles rule Israel, God never will forget His promises. Evidence lies in the fact that He led the Israelites out of their captivity and brought them back to their homeland. But why does the Lord "remember"? He remembers so that He can bless them!

The name *Berechiah*, "the Lord will bless," reminds us of God's promise to Abraham that He would, " *make of thee a great nation, and I will bless thee, and make thy name great; and thou shalt be a blessing"* (Genesis 12:2). Ultimately, the Lord will lead His people into the great blessings of the Messianic reign, as revealed in the book of Zechariah: *"And it shall come to pass, that as ye were a curse among the heathen, O house of Judah, and house of Israel; so will I save you, and ye shall be a blessing: fear not, but let your hands be strong"* (Zechariah 8:13, also compare to Isaiah 61:9). When will this be fulfilled?

The name *Iddo*, or "born at the appointed time," emphasizes that the time will come — God alone knows when — and it will not tarry (Habakkuk 2:3). God will fulfill His promise to redeem His people, bless them and make them into a blessing. The Jews will be saved at an appointed time: *"Who hath heard such a thing? who hath seen such things? Shall the earth be made to bring forth in one day? or shall a nation be born at once? for as soon as Zion travailed, she brought forth her children. Shall I bring to the birth, and not cause to bring forth? saith the LORD: shall I cause to bring forth, and shut the womb? saith thy God"* (Isaiah 66:8–9).

What does Israel's future blessing consist of? How does God remember His people? He recognizes them through His Son, Jesus Christ, which is why these three names prophetically point to Jesus.

• **Zechariah: The Lord Remembers** — Mary said the following regarding the Lord: *"He hath holpen his servant Israel, in remembrance of his mercy; As he spake to our fathers, to Abraham, and to his seed for ever"* (Luke 1:54–55).

• **Berechiah: The Lord Will Bless** — In his second sermon to the Jews following Pentecost, Peter addressed the Jewish people, saying: *"Ye are children of the prophets, and of the covenant which God made with our fathers, saying unto Abraham, And in thy seed shall all the kindreds of the earth be blessed. Unto you first God, having raised up his Son Jesus, sent him to bless you, in turning away every one of you from his iniquities"* (Acts 3:25–26).

• **Iddo: Born At An Appointed Time** — Galatians 4:4–5 contains these words regarding Christ's First Advent to earth: *"But when the fulness of the time was come, God sent forth his Son, made of a woman, made under the law, To redeem them that were under the law, that we might receive the adoption of sons."* Salvation was accomplished at Christ's First Advent through His voluntary death on the Cross and His victorious ascension. Jesus Christ is proof that God always remembers His people, that He will bless them and that He will save them. Israel's future is guaranteed because of Christ. When He returns, they will see Him whom they pierced (chapter 12:10), the time of the nations will come to an end, and He will begin His world-wide reign from Jerusalem: *"And the LORD shall be king over all the earth: in that day shall there be one LORD, and his name one"* (Zechariah 14:9).

These words also serve as a great encouragement for believers in that we, too, shall never be forgotten by God.

The Lord is before us, *"...which leadeth thee by the way"* (Isaiah 48:17).

• *"And thine ears shall hear a word behind thee, saying, This is the way, walk ye in it, when ye turn to the right hand, and when ye turn to the left"* (Isaiah 30:21).

• *"I have set the LORD always before me: because he is at my right hand, I shall not be moved"* (Psalm 16:8).

• *"On the left hand, where he doth work, but I cannot behold him: he hideth himself on the right hand, that I cannot see him"* (Job 23:9).

• *"How excellent is thy lovingkindness, O God! therefore the children of men put their trust under the shadow of thy wings"* (Psalm 36:7).

• *"The eternal God is thy refuge, and underneath are the everlasting arms: and he shall thrust out the enemy from before thee; and shall say, Destroy them"* (Deuteronomy 33:27).

- *"O LORD, thou hast searched me, and known me. Thou knowest my downsitting and mine uprising, thou understandest my thought afar off. Thou compassest my path and my lying down, and art acquainted with all my ways. For there is not a word in my tongue, but, lo, O LORD, thou knowest it altogether. Thou hast beset me behind and before, and laid thine hand upon me. Such knowledge is too wonderful for me; it is high, I cannot attain unto it"* (Psalm 139:1–6).

- *"Know ye not that ye are the temple of God, and that the Spirit of God dwelleth in you?"* (1st Corinthians 3:16). How could He forget us? In Christ we are always blessed, and He wants to make us a blessing: *"Blessed be the God and Father of our Lord Jesus Christ, who hath blessed us with all spiritual blessings in heavenly places in Christ"* (Ephesians 1:3). Jesus was born, died and rose again!

2. Encouragement Through A Promise

"The LORD hath been sore displeased with your fathers. Therefore say thou unto them, Thus saith the LORD of hosts; Turn ye unto me, saith the LORD of hosts, and I will turn unto you, saith the LORD of hosts" (Zechariah 1:2–3). The Lord was very displeased with His disobedient people in the past; subsequently, they were led into captivity (2nd Kings 21:14–15). But things were about to change. The Lord

wanted to forget His anger and turn back to them. His grace would again be upon Israel. God's demand to turn to Him was not based upon a threat of judgment, but on the promise that He would turn to them. However, one condition had to be fulfilled: The Jews had to turn to Him again with their whole hearts.

Haggai admonished the people to begin rebuilding the Temple, a task that had become neglected (Haggai 1:12–15). The Israelites listened to the Lord's voice and were encouraged to proceed with the building of the Temple. The Lord promised them: *"I am with you, saith the LORD"* (Haggai 1:13).

Two months into the rebuilding, they were admonished to give Him their hearts. Why? The Lord could have said, "How wonderful it is to see how busy you are working on My house!" Instead, He instructed them to turn to Him!

Consider this profound statement: You can serve the Lord without following Him, but you cannot follow Him without serving Him! Apparently, the Israelites were serving the Lord without following Him. They were busy working on the Temple, but the Lord wanted more. He wanted their hearts. They weren't instructed to simply work on the Temple in an attempt to outwardly fulfill the Law; the Lord wanted them to turn back to Him as well: *"Turn ye unto me!"*

God expressed this call to turn around through Hosea the prophet with these words: *"For I desired mercy, and not sacrifice; and the knowledge of God more than burnt offerings"* (Hosea 6:6). Only when Israel gave the Lord first priority would the blessings flow in full measure.

For believers, this means that our personal, earnest dedication to Jesus Christ is more important than everything we do for Him or for His Name's sake. Jesus doesn't want our service; He wants our hearts! Of course, He wants to use us as His co-workers, but what He really desires is our love. He wants to have deep fellowship with His children. The Lord blesses our hard work for Him, and we experience that He is with us in it; but we should also experience Him much more deeply. But we can only do this if we have turned wholeheartedly to Him, living our lives for Him. The New Testament teaches this very clearly:

• The Lord acknowledged and praised the laboring and patient Ephesians, but He was really wanting to be their first love, which, according to Revelation 2:1–7, was lacking.

• When the Lord chose His twelve apostles for service, He was concerned with something much more important: *"And he ordained twelve, that they should be with him, and that he might send them forth to preach"* (Mark 3:14).

• Ephesians 1:5 says that God has *"...predestinated us unto the adoption of children by Jesus Christ to himself, according to the good pleasure of his will."*

We are called and predestined according to the good pleasure of His will.

• Paul said of himself: *"For I through the law am dead to the law, that I might live unto God"* (Galatians 2:19).

Living for God, having fellowship with Jesus, and serving Him out of this fellowship is what counts. This is the essence of Christianity. Blessings for our lives and deeds are only found in our complete devotion to God.

3. Encouragement Through Reminding

"Be ye not as your fathers, unto whom the former prophets have cried, saying, Thus saith the LORD of hosts; Turn ye now from your evil ways, and from your evil doings: but they did not hear, nor hearken unto me, saith the LORD. Your fathers, where are they? and the prophets, do they live for ever? But my words and my statutes, which I commanded my servants the prophets, did they not take hold of your fathers? and they returned and said, Like as the LORD of hosts thought to do unto us, according to our ways, and according to our doings, so hath he dealt with us" (Zechariah 1:4–6).

The Lord reminded His people of past occasions when their fathers had been disobedient to Him, had not listened to Him and had committed spiritual adultery (see Ezekiel and Hosea). The Israelites thought they could cast the words of the prophets to the wind. What was the result? It was shocking! How moving that God doesn't speak about the terrible punishments that came upon His people, but about their mortality: "Your fathers, where are they?" What remained of them? What had their rebellion brought them? They had died in their sin! That is the worst thing that can possibly happen to a person!

What counts is what remains at the end of our lives. Where are the great mockers, tyrants and atheists of world history? They have all passed away, but God lives forever. His Word, in contrast to them, will abide for all eternity! How many generations have had to acknowledge that the "great" men of the past were wrong? Where is Lenin today? Where are Stalin, Hitler, Mao Tse-tung, Voltaire and Nietzsche? Millions of people looked up to them. But where are they now?

A report on Nietzsche entitled "The Way To Insanity," describes Nietzsche's last years as being characterized by sickness, headaches, eye pain and a tormenting depression. He was afraid of noise, near-sighted and had stomach trouble. He was afflicted by vomiting and a colic that led to unconsciousness. He needed more and more medication in order to sleep. Ultimately, he went insane. This man who said "no" to everything weak and "yes" to everything strong seemed to have no scruples. With words like the blows of a hammer, he turned against everything godly and made a genuine contribution with his philosophy to an atheistic way of thinking. But in the depth of his soul, he knew of the One against whom He arose. He once wrote the words, "God is dead! God will stay dead! And we have killed Him! How shall we comfort ourselves, the murderers of all murderers? The most Holy and Mighty the world possessed bled to death through our knives. Who will wipe this blood from us? With what water can we cleanse ourselves?" Nietzsche became a desperate man. He died, but God lives!

With the words of Zechariah 1:5, "...and the prophets, do they live for ever?," the Lord was surely saying that His servants were also buried, but His work continues. The prophets proclaimed the truth and died in service; yet the truth remains.

In summary, some didn't believe, died and perished, while others believed and died but remained in eternity. The Jews who returned from Babylonian captivity recognized this and turned wholeheartedly to their Lord. We will all experience death, but our trust in God, our devotion to Christ, and our service to Him will remain in eternity. Paul said, "Therefore, my beloved brethren, be ye stedfast, unmoveable, always abounding in the work of the Lord, forasmuch as ye know that your labour is not in vain in the Lord" (1st Corinthians 15:58).

CHAPTER 2

THE MAN AMONG THE MYRTLE TREES

"Upon the four and twentieth day of the eleventh month, which is the month Sebat, in the second year of Darius, came the word of the LORD unto Zechariah, the son of Berechiah, the son of Iddo the prophet, saying, I saw by night, and behold a man riding upon a red horse, and he stood among the myrtle trees that were in the bottom; and behind him were there red horses, speckled, and white. Then said I, O my lord, what are these? And the angel that talked with me said unto me, I will shew thee what these be. And the man that stood among the myrtle trees answered and said, These are they whom the LORD hath sent to walk to and fro through the earth. And they answered the angel of the LORD that stood among the myrtle trees, and said, We have walked to and fro through the earth, and, behold, all the earth sitteth still, and is at rest. Then the angel of the LORD

answered and said, O LORD of hosts, how long wilt thou not have mercy on Jerusalem and on the cities of Judah, against which thou hast had indignation these threescore and ten years? And the LORD answered the angel that talked with me with good words and comfortable words. So the angel that communed with me said unto me, Cry thou, saying, Thus saith the LORD of hosts; I am jealous for Jerusalem and for Zion with a great jealousy. And I am very sore displeased with the heathen that are at ease: for I was but a little displeased, and they helped forward the affliction. Therefore thus saith the LORD; I am returned to Jerusalem with mercies: my house shall be built in it, saith the LORD of hosts, and a line shall be stretched forth upon Jerusalem. Cry yet, saying, Thus saith the LORD of hosts; My cities through prosperity shall yet be spread abroad; and the LORD shall yet comfort Zion, and shall yet choose Jerusalem" (Zechariah 1:7–17).

Approximately three months after Zechariah instructed his people to give themselves wholly to the Lord (compare verses 1 and 7), he received this mighty vision illustrating Jerusalem's future: *"Thus saith the LORD of hosts; Turn ye unto me, saith the LORD of hosts, and I will turn unto you, saith the LORD of hosts"* (verse 3). Just how literally this promise should be taken is evident from God's first revelation concerning the future of the city.

The Jews had returned to Jerusalem. They had started to rebuild the Temple and had turned to the Lord again. God's answer was not long in coming: He turned back to them and gave them a wonderful revelation of the city of the great King (Matthew 5:35)! The curse they had been under until then would be removed, and again, they would be a blessing (Zechariah 8:13).

A large number of Jews will turn to the Lord during the Great Tribulation. According to Revelation 11:1, they will also rebuild the Temple. Then the Lord will return to His people.

God's promises will also become a perceivable blessing, comfort and living hope for those of us who believe on the Lord Jesus Christ when we dedicate ourselves completely to Him: *"Submit yourselves therefore to God...Draw nigh to God, and he will draw nigh to you"* (James 4:7–8).

Jerusalem During The Times Of The Nations

"I saw by night, and behold a man riding upon a red horse, and he stood among the myrtle trees that were in the bottom; and behind him there were red horses, speckled, and white" (Zechariah 1:8). Zechariah saw a rider on a red horse who stopped in a ravine (NIV) *"...among the myrtle trees."* The myrtle tree symbolizes Jerusalem, where many of them grow in the valleys. Characterized by their dark, green,

glossy leaves, they are adorned with flowers. During Zechariah's time, they were often used as wedding decorations and at the Feast of the Tabernacles (Nehemiah 8:15). Perfume also was made from myrtle trees.

The tree's green leaves signify Israel's hope and future. Jerusalem will not fade. It will bloom before the Lord forever.

Where were these myrtles located? In a deep ravine. Many expositors consider this to be the Kidron Valley. The "ravine" symbolizes Israel's position among the nations. The time of the Gentiles began with Jerusalem's first destruction by the Babylonians. Jerusalem never really has been free since then. Jerusalem was ruled by the Romans when Jesus was here the first time. This occupation will last until Jesus returns as Israel's Messiah: *"...and Jerusalem shall be trodden down of the Gentiles, until the times of the Gentiles be fulfilled"* (Luke 21:24).

Jerusalem (Israel) is like the myrtle tree, which grows modestly in a shady, low place. Accordingly, Israel and her people are despised by the nations even today. Jerusalem is contested and hated, and the other nations of the world would like to take the country back from the Jews.

The Nations' Thoughts

While Israel, the myrtle, is despised by the nations, the Lord stands among the myrtles in the ravine. He remains standing where others have passed by. Three times, we see reference to this:

1. *"...He stood among the myrtle trees that were in the bottom..."* (verse 8)

2. *"And the man that stood among the myrtle trees answered and said..."* (verse 10)

3. *"And they answered the angel of the LORD that stood among the myrtle trees..."* (verse 11)

While the nations treat Israel thoughtlessly, the Lord remembers them: *"And they answered the angel of the LORD that stood among the myrtle trees, and said, We have walked to and fro through the earth, and, behold, all the earth sitteth still, and is at rest"* (verse 11). As messengers of the Lord of hosts, the angels mentioned in this verse were given the task of seeing how the nations would behave toward Jerusalem. What did they see? Indifference, thoughtlessness, self-confidence and a presumptuous rest. Nobody cared about Jerusalem. Peace among the nations was more important than siding with Israel. There was no turning to the Lord and His Word; neither was there a turning to Israel.

Nothing's changed. The world remains relatively silent when terrorists murder Jewish women and children. Similarly, there is no protest when the Arab League and its representatives pour out their tirades of hatred on Israel. Hardly anyone lifts a finger in response to these injustices toward Israel. But the same world condemns Israel every time she makes a move — even when she is defending herself!

How different were the Lord's thoughts? Jerusalem is mentioned 5 times in this passage of Zechariah. God's feelings about the city are apparent:

• *"Then the angel of the LORD answered and said, O LORD of hosts, how long wilt thou not have mercy on Jerusalem and on the cities of Judah, against which thou hast had indignation these threescore and ten years"* (verse 12)

• *"Thus saith the LORD of hosts; I am jealous for Jerusalem and for Zion with a great jealousy"* (verse 14)

• *"Therefore thus saith the LORD; I am returned to Jerusalem with mercies: my house shall be built in it, saith the LORD of hosts, and a line shall be stretched forth upon Jerusalem"* (verse 16)

• *"Cry yet, saying, Thus saith the LORD of hosts; My cities through prosperity shall yet be spread abroad; and the LORD shall yet comfort Zion, and shall yet choose Jerusalem"* (verse 17)

Who among the mighty men of our world has like-minded thoughts concerning Jerusalem? This shows how far the nations live from the thoughts of God. The Lord is on Jerusalem's side, even if the nations are indifferent and thoughtless. The number 5 represents grace. The day will come when the Lord turns to Jerusalem again in all His perfect grace. He will have mercy upon His city and people; He will again be jealous for them; He will comfort them and He will choose them.

Final Solution Or Final Liberation?

"And I am very sore displeased with the heathen that are at ease: for I was but a little displeased, and they helped forward the affliction" (verse 15). The nations are eagerly searching for a final solution to the Jewish question. God punished His people, but the nations have never acted in accordance with His will. A "final solution" will never be justified; therefore, the answer to such an attempt will always be divine wrath. The Lord doesn't want a final solution, He wants Israel's final liberation from the pressure of the nations. This final liberation will come when Jesus returns. Then, His thoughts against all the nations but Jerusalem will be realized. The time of the Gentiles will end. God's wrath will come upon the nations in such fury that they will cry: *"And the kings of the earth, and the great men, and the rich men, and the chief captains, and the mighty men, and every bondman, and every free man, hid themselves in the dens and in the rocks of the mountains; And said to the mountains and rocks, Fall on us, and hide us from the face of him that sitteth on the throne, and from the wrath of the Lamb: For the great day of his wrath is come; and who shall be able to stand?"* (Revelation 6:15–17).

We must not be indifferent where Jerusalem is concerned. The land of Israel and the Jewish people must be dear to our hearts because they are dear to the Lord. It is not by chance that Zechariah was told twice that he should proclaim the words of the Lord: *"So the angel that communed with me said unto me, Cry thou, saying, Thus saith the LORD of hosts; I am jealous for Jerusalem and for Zion with a great jealousy"* (Zechariah 1:14) and, *"Cry yet, saying, Thus saith the LORD of hosts; My cities through prosperity shall yet be spread abroad; and the LORD shall yet comfort Zion, and shall yet choose Jerusalem"* (verse 17). The Lord is angry with those who hate Jerusalem, but He will bless those who love her: *"Pray for the peace of Jerusalem: they shall prosper that love thee"* (Psalm 122:6).

The One Who Turns Everything Around

"I saw by night, and behold a man riding upon a red horse, and he stood among the myrtle trees that were in the bottom; and behind him were there red horses, speckled, and white" (Zechariah 1:8). Who is this mysterious man who stands among the myrtle trees? It is the Son of man, Jesus Christ, Israel's Messiah! He is concerned about Jerusalem, and He is also concerned about you!

The man among the myrtle trees appears suddenly on a red horse during the time of the nations, in the middle of the night (verse 8). Israel had no king at that time. The Jews were busy rebuilding Jerusalem, and were encountering violent resistance from their enemies. Even at that time, the Arabs were contesting their right to Jerusalem: *"Now it came to pass, when Sanballat, and Tobiah, and Geshem the Arabian, and the rest of our enemies, heard that I had builded the wall, and that there was no breach left therein; (though at that time I had not set up the doors upon the gates;)..."* (Nehemiah 6:1). It's no different today! The Arabs have been raging against Israel since Jerusalem has been reclaimed by Israel. Pressure from Jerusalem's enemies is increasing. The city's enemies are not only Arabs, but are also found in other nations around the world. This will continue until the end of the days when all the nations will gather against Jerusalem. Then Jerusalem will become a cup of trembling (Zechariah 12:2). When the city of Jerusalem is at its lowest point ever, the Lord will take care of His people, who are despised by the world. The Lord's return will bring about Israel's salvation, light and blessing.

Why does the Lord stand between the myrtles? It may be a prophetic reference to Isaiah 55:13: *"Instead of the thorn shall come up the fir tree, and instead of the brier shall come up the myrtle tree: and it shall be to the LORD for a name, for an everlasting sign that shall not be cut off."*

Blessing Instead Of Cursing — Life Instead Of Death

The Lord, who bore a crown of thorns, and over whose head was written, *"Jesus of Nazareth the king of the Jews"* (John 19:19), will see that the curse is removed and that myrtles grow in the place of thorns. He who bore the curse of the crown of thorns in His death now stands among the myrtles because Jerusalem will flourish eternally before Him and through Him. The Lord stands by Jerusalem. This time He will wear a crown of ornaments instead of a crown of thorns: *"I will greatly rejoice in the LORD, my soul shall be joyful in my God; for he hath clothed me with the garments of salvation, he hath covered me with the robe of righteousness, as a bridegroom decketh himself with ornaments, and as a bride adorneth herself with her jewels"* (Isaiah 61:10).

Let's return to the fact that the man is standing among the myrtles in the ravine (verse 8). Where is the lowest point of the earth's surface? Geographically, it is the Dead Sea, but spiritually, it is Calvary. The Lord descended from heaven to earth to reconcile the world to God. Israel's future salvation also lies in Calvary: *"...he humbled himself, and became obedient unto death, even the death of the cross"* (Philippians 2:8). He stands in the ravine among the myrtle trees to bring salvation to His people. While the world stands against Israel, the Lord Himself will stand by Jerusalem!

This man who appears on the scene is riding a red horse. Red symbolizes the color of His blood, the color of victory; but it also represents the color of the Judge over all the nations. Here, this man is called *"the angel of the Lord." "And they answered the angel of the LORD that stood among the myrtle trees, and said, We have walked to and fro through the earth, and, behold, all the earth sitteth still, and is at rest"* (Zechariah 1:11). Clearly, it is the Lord Himself who stands among the myrtle trees. The term *"angel of the Lord"* often refers to the preincarnate Lord Jesus Christ who is synonymous with God (Genesis 22:15–17). He is the visible manifestation of the invisible God in the Old Testament.

Who Can Bring The Gospel Message To The People?

Only the Lord can bring the Gospel message to the people. An angel spoke to Zechariah in verse 9. Zechariah asked the angel about the horse's significance: *"Then said I, O my lord, what are these? And the angel that talked with me said unto me, I will shew thee what these be."* The angel wanted to answer him, but apparently he could not. He could only point to the One with the answer, the Lord as the angel of the Lord: *"And the man that stood among the myrtle trees answered and said, These are they whom the LORD hath sent to walk to and fro through the earth"* (verse 10). Jesus is the only One who can answer the most important questions in life.

A great biblical truth is revealed: Whom and what Jesus Christ is in His work of redemption. Peter wrote, *"...the things, which are now reported unto you by them that have preached the gospel unto you with the Holy Ghost sent down from heaven; which things the angels desire to look into"* (1st Peter 1:12). Even the angels would like to reverently look into the work of salvation through Jesus in all its glory, but they are unable because they are sinless beings who have no need for salvation. However, the Lord proclaims the message of life to us through His Word by means of the Holy Spirit. And this Lord wants to speak to our hearts right now.

Behind the man among the myrtles stands God's heavenly host. The angels on the red, speckled and white horses show us that over the visible armies of this world is an invisible host of God which is much mightier: *"And he answered, Fear not: for they that be with us are more than they that be with them"* (2nd Kings 6:16, compare also to Revelation 12:7–9). The significance of the different colors is not explained, but the colors are certainly apocalyptic.

This Lord who once wept over Jerusalem will now stand as a High Priest and Advocate for Jerusalem and Judah, and He prays for them: *"Then the angel of the LORD answered and said, O LORD of hosts, how long wilt thou not have mercy on Jerusalem and on the cities of Judah, against which thou hast had in-dignation these threescore and ten years? And the LORD answered the angel that talked with me with good words and comfortable words"* (Zechariah 1:12–13). If the Lord Himself intercedes for Jerusalem and Judah in such a moving way, should we love Israel any less? It is very comforting to know that someone is praying for Jerusalem. Scripture does not reveal what the Father said to the Son, but He must have used kind, comforting words, for we know that the Father always hears the Son (John 11:42 and John 17), and doubtless He did so in this case as well.

The timing of Jerusalem's final restoration is not mentioned anywhere in the Bible. It will take place when Jesus returns. Nobody knows the day or hour this will take place. Although we are not told when it will take place, we are told how. Following His prayer and God's response, the Lord turned back to Zechariah and commanded him to cry aloud for Jerusalem, making it clear that He had been heard, and that they must have been wonderful words (verse 13 onward). For with all divine authority it is to be proclaimed that the time is coming when the Lord will turn back to His people.

What Is The Message That All Should Hear?

Let's summarize the seven statements concerning Jerusalem:

1. *"I am jealous for Jerusalem and for Zion with*

a great jealousy"

– The divine authority — God Himself — is with Jerusalem.

2. *"I am returned to Jerusalem with mercies"*

– The divine love is of Jerusalem.

3. *"My house shall be built in it"*

– The divine presence is back in Jerusalem.

4. *"A line shall be stretched forth upon Jerusalem"* (Jeremiah 31:38–40)

– The divine indivisibility remains in Jerusalem.

5. *"My cities through prosperity shall yet be spread abroad"*

– The divine blessing is back in Jerusalem.

6. *"The Lord shall yet comfort Zion"*

– The divine kindness is back in Jeruslaem.

7. *"...And shall yet choose Jerusalem"*

– The divine promise will remain in Jerusalem.

And, concerning the nations, we read:

8. *"I am very sore displeased with the heathen..."*

– The divine wrath will fall over all those who hate Jerusalem.

CHAPTER 3

THE LAST SMITH IN
WORLD HISTORY

"Then lifted I up mine eyes, and saw, and behold four horns. And I said unto the angel that talked with me, What be these? And he answered me, These are the horns which have scattered Judah, Israel, and Jerusalem. And the LORD shewed me four carpenters. Then said I, What come these to do? And he spake, saying, These are the horns which have scattered Judah, so that no man did lift up his head: but these are come to fray them, to cast out the horns of the Gentiles, which lifted up their horn over the land of Judah to scatter it" (Zechariah 1:18–21).

The devil despises God's promises concerning Israel and the Church. He intended to prevent the Messiah's birth in Bethlehem. But as we know, he failed to do that, neither will he be able to prevent Jesus' return in great power and glory to set up His kingdom in Israel. At His First Advent, Jesus conquered the devil and redeemed the world on Calvary's Cross. At His Second Coming, He will destroy the anti-Christian empire. Won't you accompany me on a trip through one of the most fascinating chapters in the Bible?

It seems as though these four horns heard what the Lord had promised Israel, and now they are doing all they can to prevent this promise from being fulfilled. It wasn't the four horns, but Satan, the one who leads them, that overheard. He knows Jerusalem's future and has been using the nations to resist God's plan for centuries. This is Satan's battle against the One who promised to choose Jerusalem again.

As the prince and god of the nations, Satan will lead an assault against Israel (Ephesians 2:2). He was behind the Pharaoh of Egypt in the destruction of Israel, because he didn't want the Jews to reach the Promised Land. Isaiah writes: *"Awake, awake, put on strength, O arm of the LORD; awake, as in the ancient days, in the generations of old. Art though not it that hath cut Rahab, and wounded the dragon? Art thou not it which hath dried the sea, the waters of the great deep; that hath made the depths of the sea a way for the ransomed to pass over? Therefore the redeemed of the LORD shall return, and come with singing unto Zion; and everlasting joy shall be upon their head: they shall obtain gladness and joy; and sorrow and mourning shall flee away"* (Isaiah 51:9–11).

This same dragon will also oppose Israel in the

endtimes, with the intention of destroying God's promises and preventing Jesus' return: *"And when the dragon saw that he was cast unto the earth, he persecuted the woman which brought forth the man child"* (Revelation 12:13). *"And the dragon was wroth with the woman, and went to make war with the remnant of her seed, which keep the commandments of God, and have the testimony of Jesus Christ"* (Revelation 12:17). In more recent history, we see how the dragon has used the nations to oppose Israel. Who was behind the Inquisition? Who was behind the Holocaust? Who is behind Islam?

The Prophet's Watchfulness

The Lord gave Zechariah this revelation during the night. The prophet *"...lifted up his eyes and saw."* This action illustrates a continuous watchfulness in the middle of the night. We are living in the evening of spiritual history; the night around us is growing darker. That is why we are required to watch. God wants to reveal His plan for the endtimes to His children. If we are spiritually asleep, then we will dream right through the spiritual events of our time. The Lord had a reason for saying this to His disciples, *"...what I say unto you I say unto all, Watch"* (Mark 13:37). It is very important that we concern ourselves with the prophetic Word of the Bible and try to understand its meaning just as Daniel did in his time, *"And he*

(Gabriel) *informed me, and talked with me, and said, O Daniel, I am now come forth to give thee skill and understanding"* (Daniel 9:22). Zechariah was the type of man who immediately asked for an explanation when he didn't understand something, *"...I said unto the angel that talked with me, What be these?"* (Zechariah 1:19).

Daniel did the same thing with his friends: *"Then Daniel went to his house, and made the thing known to Hananiah, Mishael, and Azariah, his companions: That they would desire mercies of the God of heaven concerning this secret; that Daniel and his fellows should not perish with the rest of the wise men of Babylon. Then was the secret revealed unto Daniel in a night vision. Then Daniel blessed the God of heaven"* (Daniel 2:17–19). Revelation 1:3 records: *"Blessed is he that readeth, and they that hear the words of this prophecy, and keep those things which are written therein: for the time is at hand."*

The Four Horns And Their Meaning

The four horns symbolize the nations' endless enmity against Judah, Israel and Jerusalem. Horns in the Bible represent power. They indicate invincible strength and political power (Micah 4:13, Revelation 13:1 and 17:12, Daniel 7:24, 8:8–9 and 20–22). In Zechariah's case, they also symbolize the power of the nations that are against Israel: *"These are the horns which have scattered Judah, Israel, and Jerusalem"* (Zechariah 1:19).

Who Do The Horns Represent?

The horns also represent the four world Empires — Babylon, Persia, Greece and Rome. During Zechariah's time, the prophet could only imagine two world Empires; Babylon and Persia. Yet, in chapter 9:13, he speaks of Greece, which was still a few centuries in the future. And he also saw Rome follow Greece. Zechariah recognized that Satan will continue to oppose and oppress Israel through hostile nations so that the Lord should by no means rule in Jerusalem as He has promised (Zechariah 1:12–17).

The Jews clung to Jerusalem during the centuries of their dispersion. Countless Jews died far from their homeland, but their hearts were nonetheless in Jerusalem. "Next year in Jerusalem" remained their hope. This hope is expressed by the words in Psalm 137:5–6, *"If I forget thee, O Jerusalem, let my right hand forget her cunning. If I do not remember thee, let my tongue cleave to the roof of my mouth; if I prefer not Jerusalem above my chief joy."*

The four horns also represent the nations' worldwide hostility toward Israel, because the number four can also represent the four directions: north, south, east and west. Israel is hated all over the world because the world is under the dragon's rule. The Jews have always been surrounded by a threatening world.

Zechariah wrote that one day, all of the nations would attack the Jews, and that all of the nations would gather against Jerusalem (Zechariah 12:2–3). The Bible leaves no doubt that all the nations will focus on Israel, and that this will take place at Armageddon: *"For they are the spirits of devils, working miracles, which go forth unto the kings of the earth and of the whole world, to gather them to the battle of that great day of God Almighty"* (Revelation 16:14). According to Revelation chapter 17, the nations will give their power to this one horn, the Antichrist, and, inspired by the dragon, he will lead the nations into war against Israel. Yet nothing and nobody, neither in heaven nor on earth, nor under the earth that will be able to destroy God's promises to His people.

The Four Smiths

The Amplified Bible translates the Hebrew word in Zechariah 1:20 as "smiths" or "workmen." In Psalm 75:10 the Lord said, *"All the horns of the wicked also will I cut off; but the horns of the righteous shall be exalted"* (Psalm 75:10). The "smiths" will be used by God to terrify the horns and cut them off. How will it be done? How will it happen? The four "smiths" oppose the four horns. Isaiah 54:16 says, *"Behold, I have created the smith that bloweth the coals in the fire, and that bringeth forth an instrument for his work; and I have created the waster to destroy"* (Isaiah 54:16). In days past, the Lord used individual world empires to destroy the one preceding it. He did this for a very specific reason recorded in Zechariah 1:15: *"And I am very sore displeased with the heathen that are at ease: for I was but a little displeased, and they helped forward the affliction."*

Persia–The First Smith–Destroyed Babylon

Persia's King Cyrus was created by God Himself as a smith and was destined to conquer Babylon. God's infinite wisdom, power and love for Israel is revealed in these words: *"Thus saith the LORD to his anointed, to Cyrus, whose right hand I have holden, to subdue nations before him; and I will loose the loins of kings, to open for before him the two leaved gates; and the gates shall not be shut; I will go before thee, and make the crooked places straight: I will break in pieces the gates of brass, and cut in sunder the bars of iron: And I will give thee the treasures of darkness, and hidden riches of secret places, that thou mayest know that I, the LORD, which call thee by thy name, am the God of Israel. For Jacob my servant's sake, and Israel mine elect, I have even called thee by thy name: I have surnamed thee, though thou hast not known me"* (Isaiah 45:1–4). Cyrus conquered Babylon and gave Israel the freedom to return to Jerusalem. About 200 years before Cyrus, God called him by his name and said of him: *"...He is my shepherd, and shall perform all my pleasure: even saying to Jerusalem, Thou shalt be built; and to the temple, Thy foundation shall be laid"* (Isaiah 44:28). That is exactly what happened! The Lord chose in Cyrus a smith to terrify the horn of Babylon and cut it off. Daniel 5:6 describes how the Babylonian king was reduced to fear and trembling on the night Persia attacked and conquered him. In the time following Cyrus, Persia suffered a defeat and the Empire opposed Israel. Then the Lord awakened another smith.

Greece – The Second Smith – Overcame Persia

Alexander the Great is mentioned particularly in Daniel 7:6 and 8:5. His kingdom is described in chapters 2, 7 and 8 as Persia's successor. It is said that Alexander the Great treated the Jews in a friendly manner, but after his early death, the Empire was divided and it ended up opposing Israel. This took place mainly under King Antiochus Epiphanes, who came from Syria and who is mentioned in Daniel chapter 8. Subsequently, God awakened another smith who cut off the horn of Greece and broke its power.

Rome – The Third Smith – Overcame Greece

Rome, which is mentioned in Daniel 2, 7, 8 and in the book of Revelation, was the mightiest Empire as well as the one that lasted the longest. The Romans ruled Israel when Jesus was born, and destroyed Jerusalem in 70 A.D. Julius Caesar was Rome's first, and probably greatest, leader. Rome's fall did not transpire through a smith taking over world rulership as with the preceding Empires. Rather, Rome experienced an inner decay; it degenerated, lost wars, divided itself and eventually fell. Why didn't it suffer the same fate as the Empires before it? The Bible explains (see Revelation 17:8 and 11) that Rome didn't fall indefinitely, but that its hour has not yet come. Rome will experience a new revival in the endtimes and will become the last world Empire with ten horns. It will introduce the political Antichrist. All of the preceding Empires will be united in this last world Empire (Revelation 13:1–2), and all the nations will turn against Israel and attempt to destroy her. But this Empire will only be destroyed by Jesus' return (Revelation 17:14).

Jesus Is The Fourth Smith

Jesus Himself will conquer the anti-Christian empire. We read of Him and His future in Daniel 2:44: *"And in the days of these kings shall the God of heaven set up a kingdom, which shall never be destroyed: and the kingdom shall not be left to other people, but it shall break in pieces and consume all these kingdoms, and it shall stand for ever."* We see that the Lord Jesus is like a smith by His statement to all the nations in His future kingdom to turn their swords into plowshares and their spears into pruning hooks (Isaiah 2:4). But He will lead His people to a special place.

The Four Horns Of Grace

Exodus 27:1–2 says: *"And thou shalt make an altar of shittim wood...And thou shalt make the horns of it upon the four corners thereof: his horns shall be of the same: and thou shalt overlay it with brass."* This was the brazen altar upon which the whole burnt offering was sacrificed. It points to Calvary, where Jesus died for His people. These four horns of the altar symbolize God's superior power compared to all other world powers. The power of forgiveness is stronger than the power of sin, and it reaches to the ends of the earth.

Atonement was to be accomplished once a year on the horns of this altar with the blood of the sin offering for the people of Israel: *"And Aaron shall make an atonement upon the horns of it once in a year with the blood of the sin offering of atonements: once in the year shall he make atonement upon it throughout your generations: it is most holy unto the LORD"* (Exodus 30:10). Israel's great day of atonement is not far off. She will grasp the four horns of grace and forgiveness and look upon the sacrifice (Zechariah 12:10)! Exodus 29:37 says: *"...whatsoever toucheth the altar shall be holy."* The people will then receive forgiveness and holiness. All of this will take place in one single day: *"...I will remove the iniquity of that land in one day"*

(Zechariah 3:9). Zechariah 14:20 says, "*In that day shall there be upon the bells of the horses, HOLINESS UNTO THE LORD; and the pots in the LORD's house shall be like the bowls before the altar.*" The Lord will achieve His goal with Israel and His Church. The gates of hell will not prevail against them, for the rulers of this world will pass away, but Jesus Christ is coming back!

CHAPTER 4

WHO WILL HAVE THE LAST WORD CONCERNING JERUSALEM?

"I lifted up mine eyes again, and looked, and behold a man with a measuring line in his hand. Then said I, Whither goest thou? And he said unto me, To measure Jerusalem, to see what is the breadth thereof, and what is the length thereof. And, behold, the angel that talked with me went forth, and another angel went out to meet him, And said unto him, Run, speak to this young man, saying, Jerusalem shall be inhabited as towns without walls for the multitude of men and cattle therein: For I, saith the LORD, will be unto her a wall of fire round about, and will be the glory in the midst of her. Ho, ho, come forth, and flee from the land of the north, saith the LORD: for I have spread you abroad as the four winds of the heaven, saith the LORD. Deliver thyself, O Zion, that dwellest with the daughter of Babylon. For thus saith the LORD of hosts; After the glory hath he sent me

unto the nations which spoiled you: for he that toucheth you toucheth the apple of his eye. For, behold, I will shake mine hand upon them, and they shall be a spoil to their servants: know that the LORD of hosts hath sent me. Sing and rejoice, O daughter of Zion: for, lo, I come, and I will dwell in the midst of thee, saith the LORD. And many nations shall be joined to the LORD in that day, and shall be my people: and I will dwell in the midst of thee, and thou shalt know the LORD of hosts hath sent me unto thee. And the LORD shall inherit Judah his portion in the holy land, and shall choose Jerusalem again. Be silent, O all flesh, before the LORD: for he is raised up out of his holy habitation" (Zechariah 2:1–13).

The most important of all political questions today is this: To whom does the city of Jerusalem belong? The Jews? The Arabs? Or both? East Jerusalem was under Jordanian rule until 1967. Jordan had simply annexed this part of the city. Then East Jerusalem was conquered by the Israelis during the Six-Day War in 1967, and finally was declared the indivisible capital of Israel by the Knesset, the Israeli parliament, in 1982. As a result, a number of states moved their embassies from Jerusalem to Tel Aviv.

The political discussions taking place between the rulers of this world and the battle of the Palestinians are clearly aimed at dividing Jerusalem into two capitals. The United Nations is also in favor of a division, and leading Muslims are even claiming all of Jerusalem for the Arab world.

Who will have the last word concerning Jerusalem? The answer is clear from the Bible text quoted above: *"And the LORD shall inherit Judah his portion in the holy land, and shall choose Jerusalem again. Be silent, O all flesh, before the LORD: for he is raised up out of his holy habitation"* (Zechariah 2:12–13). God's words are vitally significant concerning a solution to the Middle East question. It couldn't be any more clear that the Lord will have the last word and the nations will be silenced. However loudly they may rant and rave today, the fact remains: Jerusalem is God's concern! The Lord's words in this chapter put an end to all speculation concerning Israel and Jerusalem.

The Man With The Measuring Line

"I lifted up mine eyes again, and looked, and behold a man with a measuring line in his hand" (Zechariah 2:1). The first thing the Lord showed Zechariah was a man with a measuring line with which to measure Jerusalem. This measuring line was already mentioned in chapter 1:16. Who is this man with the measuring line? What does this prophetic act say to us? It seems that Jesus Himself is portrayed here. Ezekiel mentioned a similar person: *"In the visions of God brought he me into the land of Israel, and set me upon a very high mountain, by which was*

as the frame of a city on the south. And he brought me thither, and, behold, there was a man, whose appearance was like the appearance of brass, with a line of flax in his hand, and a measuring reed; and he stood in the gate" (Ezekiel 40:2–3). Ezekiel 1:26–27 describes this man even more clearly: *"And above the firmament that was over their heads was the likeness of a throne, as the appearance of a sapphire stone: and upon the likeness of the throne was the likeness as the appearance of a man above upon it. And I saw as the colour of amber, as the appearance of fire round about within it, from the appearance of his loins even upward, and from the appearance of his loins even downward, I saw as it were the appearance of fire, and it had brightness round about"* (compare with Revelation 1:12–15). Despite the threats around us, we must turn our eyes upon Jesus, the Man who is the full measure of our redemption Who has clothed us with His salvation. It was part of God's plan that the Lord Jesus grew up as the son of a carpenter; we can safely assume that He learned this trade (Matthew 13:55). The Greek word for "carpenter" is *tektoon*, which means "builder who works with wood and stone." Part of the work of such a craftsman includes measuring an object to make calculations before construction: *"The carpenter stretcheth out his rule; he marketh it out with a line; he fitteth it with planes, and he marketh it out with a compass"* (Isaiah 44:13). Did

Zechariah perhaps see the "son of a carpenter" referred to in the Gospels? He alone is capable of recognizing and portraying the exact contours of God's counsel concerning Israel and the Church.

The Measuring Line: A Symbol Of Rebuilding

In the text from Ezekiel 40:2–3 onwards, the measuring line is used for the preparation of rebuilding Jerusalem and the Temple, and therewith, for the age of the kingdom. This is just what Zechariah chapter 2 is speaking of. It's not about destruction, but about rebuilding; it is not about division, but about uniting. By measuring it, the Lord stakes His claim to Jerusalem; He is making it visible to all the enemies.

The Measuring Line: A Symbol Of Indivisibility

Consider the following Bible verses:

• *"And he hath cast the lot for them, and his hand hath divided it unto them by line: they shall possess it for ever, from generation to generation shall they dwell therein"* (Isaiah 34:17). The measuring line is a picture of the Jews' eternal claim to the land of Israel.

• *"Judgment also will I lay to the line, and righteousness to the plummet"* (Isaiah 28:17). The Lord does not base His actions on the opinion of politicians or the media. Nor is He swayed by the doctrines of a religion, or of the writings in the Koran. His measuring line is His promise to Abraham, Isaac, Jacob and David. God's justice does not allow Him to forget these promises.

• *"Behold, I have graven thee upon the palms of my hands; thy walls are continually before me"* (Isaiah 49:16). This Lord has measured Jerusalem and measured the walls around her and they are continually before Him.

The Measuring Line: A Symbol Of Protection

In the book of Revelation we see how the Temple and altar are measured in order to protect those who worship therein, *"And there was given me a reed like unto a rod: and the angel stood, saying, Rise, and measure the temple of God, and the altar, and them that worship therein. But the court which is without the temple leave out, and measure it not; for it is given unto the Gentiles: and the holy city shall they tread under foot forty and two months"* (Revelation 11:1–2). Also clear from Zechariah 2:4–5 is that we are concerned with God's protection and right to Jerusalem. The Lord protects the city both inside and out. Jesus is coming again in glory and He will set up His kingdom and make Jerusalem its center.

Today, the battle is over Jerusalem. The city is to be divided, taken from the Jews and given to the Arabs. However, God's answer is the exact opposite: The city is measured in order to be rebuilt. She exists because of the Son of God, Jesus Christ, who, at His Incarnation, came from the house of a carpenter. As far as

God is concerned, Jerusalem is indivisible.

Our lives are also "measured" and we are protected by God, however much the enemy rages, stakes his claim to our lives, breaks into our family and wants to erase our borders. We may know, however, that we are included in God's building. The enemy has no claim to us if we have received Jesus into our lives, *"Jesus Christ...In whom all the building fitly framed together groweth unto an holy temple in the LORD: In whom ye also are builded together for an habitation of God through the Spirit"* (Ephesians 2:20–22). Our lives are embedded in the whole measure of His love and are protected in this. This measure is described in Ephesians 3:17–21: *"...that ye...May be able to comprehend with all saints what is the breadth, and length, and depth, and height; And to know the love of Christ, which passeth knowledge, that ye might be filled with all the fulness of God. Now unto him that is able to do exceeding abundantly above all that we ask or think, according to the power that worketh in us, Unto him be glory in the church by Christ Jesus throughout all ages, world without end. Amen."*

Israel's Gathering And God's Judgment Upon The Nations

"Ho, ho, come forth, and flee from the land of the north, saith the LORD: for I have spread you abroad as the four winds of the heaven, saith the LORD. De-

liver thyself, O Zion, that dwellest with the daughter of Babylon. For thus saith the LORD of hosts; After the glory hath he sent me unto the nations which spoiled you: for he that toucheth you toucheth the apple of his eye. For, behold, I will shake mine hand upon them, and they shall be a spoil to their servants; and ye shall know that the LORD of hosts hath sent me" (Zechariah 2:6–9). Zechariah 2:6–7 contains a two-fold meaning: It refers to that time and offered a call to the Jews who had not returned to Israel from Babylon: "Deliver thyself, O Zion, that dwellest with the daughter of Babylon" (verse 7). Babylon is called the "land of the north" because the Babylonians and all other enemies of Jerusalem always attacked from the north. Although the Persian king made it possible for the Jews to return to their land, many of them had not taken advantage of this opportunity; they were to become the ones to receive the Messiah at His First Advent.

Today, the Jews are being led back from their second dispersion with the same goal. They are to be prepared to receive the returning Messiah. The words, "I have spread you abroad as the four winds of the heaven, saith the Lord," seem to refer to this. It is interesting to note that the first people to return to Israel around 1870 came from the north. Subsequently, they came from all four directions. The nations reacted to the Jews' second homecoming with the plundering of

Israel. They contest their right to the land and want to divide Jerusalem. This will bring the judgment upon them, referred to in verse 8.

Jesus referred to the world-wide dispersion of 70 A.D. when He said, *"And they shall fall by the edge of the sword, and shall be lead away captive into all nations: and Jerusalem shall be trodden down of the Gentiles, until the times of the Gentiles be fulfilled"* (Luke 21:24). This is the time when God will judge the nations, ending with the Great Tribulation. That is why verses 6–9 refer beyond that time to the remnant of Jews who have to flee from the anti-Christian Babylon in the Great Tribulation. This is written in Revelation 18:4: *"And I heard another voice from heaven, saying, Come out of her, my people, that ye be not partakers of her sins, and that ye receive not of her plagues."*

God's judgment will hit the nations of anti-Christian Babylon with great severity because they have laid their hands upon Israel. They have plundered the people and land and, according to Joel 3:2, they want to divide the land in their arrogant quest for power. However, the one who holds the measuring line, the One who has declared Jerusalem as His possession, will call upon them to account. Whoever attacks the honor of the Jewish people also attacks God's honor, whoever touches God's people also touches the apple of His eye. The phrase "apple of the eye" (see

Deuteronomy 32:8–10) refers to the pupil, the center and most vulnerable part of our vision. Can there be a more fitting example for God's identification with His people? God's promises regarding Israel are so closely united with Himself that every blow against Israel hits Him.

The nations have treated Israel like a servant. Now, according to verse 13, they will become the spoil of this servant. The time will come when the relationships of power in this world are turned around: *"And the people shall take them, and bring them to their place: and the house of Israel shall possess them in the land of the LORD for servants and handmaids: and they shall take them captives, whose captives they were; and they shall rule over their oppressors"* (Isaiah 14:2). Israel, who was a servant to the nations for thousands of years, will now be exalted as the head of the nations in the kingdom of Christ.

It is similar with the Church: Sin once ruled over us, but now that Jesus has redeemed us, we can rule over sin (Romans 5:21). We were servants of sin; now we are free. The tables will be turned in the future kingdom of Christ. The once persecuted, despised Church of Jesus Christ will rule with Jesus as kings and priests.

The Mysterious Speaker

Who is this mysterious person who lifts up his voice? *"For thus saith the LORD of hosts; After the glory hath he sent me unto the nations which spoiled you: for he that toucheth you toucheth the apple of his eye. For, behold, I will shake mine hand upon them, and they shall be a spoil to their servants: and ye shall know that the LORD of hosts hath sent me"* (Zechariah 2:8–9). Let's also ask ourselves: Who will appear in the "glory of God" (Matthew 24:30)? Who allows Himself to be sent to the nations for the sake of God's glory (Luke 2:32)? Who is made a Judge over the nations (John 5:22 and Matthew 25:32)? Who should they recognize as the One God sent (Luke 10:16)? It is Jesus Christ! And as our text points to the Messianic Age, no one but the Messiah Himself could be meant here. God knows the day in which His people will realize who He sent to them!

The Lord is also the *"...LORD of hosts"* (verse 8) and speaks here many times in the first person. This is the Messiah's self-confession to His people. Wasn't it He who had Nathanael (whom He called a true Israelite) in mind when He said to him, *"Before that Philip called thee, when thou wast under the fig tree, I saw thee. Nathanael answered and saith unto him, Rabbi, thou art the Son of God; thou art the King of Israel"* (John 1:48–49). God has not lost sight of His people and one day, they will join in Nathanael's confession.

The Lord Will Have The Last Word Concerning Jerusalem

"Sing and rejoice, O daughter of Zion: for, lo, I

come, *and I will dwell in the midst of thee, saith the LORD. And many nations shall be joined in the LORD in that day, and shall be my people: and I will dwell in the midst of thee, and thou shalt know that the LORD of hosts hath sent me unto thee. And the LORD shall inherit Judah his portion in the holy land, and shall choose Jerusalem again. Be silent, O all flesh, before the LORD: for he is raised up out of his holy habitation*" (Zechariah 2:10–13).

Jesus will return and will turn again to Jerusalem. He calls the city "...*daughter of Zion,*" expressing His compassion for His people. He will arise in His heavenly abode to enter into the Temple of the earthly Jerusalem. His promise, "...*lo, I come, and I will dwell in the midst of thee, saith the LORD*" (Zechariah 2:10), will be realized in five stages:

1. He dwelt among His people through the tabernacle and later in the Temple.

2. God dwelt among men when Christ came into the world: "*And the Word was made flesh, and dwelt among us*" (John 1:14).

3. Through Christ's death, resurrection and ascension, and since Pentecost, the Holy Spirit lives in the hearts of all born-again believers (John 14:23 and 1st Corinthians 3:16).

4. Following the Rapture, the Lord will dwell in Spirit among the remnant of His people by sealing them (Revelation 7).

5. Finally, the Lord will return visibly, and in glory, to live in the midst of His people (Zechariah 2:5 and 13).

There is no greater joy and no more meaningful a life than the life containing the presence of Jesus Christ. The Lord will dwell beyond Israel and Jerusalem, amongst all the nations (Zechariah 2:11). Many nations will be joined to Him. Then it will be fulfilled: *"And I heard a great voice out of heaven saying, Behold, the tabernacle of God is with men, and he will dwell with them, and they shall be his people, and God himself shall be with them, and be their God"* (Revelation 21:3). As a result, all men will become silent and not be able to say anything negative about Israel or Jerusalem. Her greatest Advocate, introduced in Zechariah 3, has taken a seat and will have the last word (Zechariah 2:12–13). Incidentally, this is the only text in the Bible describing Israel as the "holy land," for this will only be the case when Jesus returns to set up His kingdom.

CHAPTER   5

ISRAEL'S COMPLETE RESTORATION

"And he shewed me Joshua the high priest stand-
ing before the angel of the LORD, and Satan standing
at his right hand to resist him. And the LORD said
unto Satan, The LORD rebuke thee, O Satan; even
the LORD that hath chosen Jerusalem rebuke thee: is
not this a brand plucked out of the fire? Now Joshua
was clothed with filthy garments, and stood before the
angel. And he answered and spake unto those that
stood before him, saying, Take away the filthy gar-
ments from him. And unto him he said, Behold, I have
caused thine iniquity to pass from thee, and I will
clothe thee with change of raiment. And I said, Let
them set a fair mitre upon his head. So they set a fair
mitre upon his head, and clothed him with garments.
And the angel of the LORD stood by. And the angel
of the LORD protested unto Joshua, saying, Thus
saith the LORD of hosts; If thou wilt walk in my
ways, and if thou wilt keep my charge, then thou shalt

also judge my house, and shalt also keep my courts, and I will give thee places to walk among these that stand by. Hear now, O Joshua the high priest, thou, and thy fellows that sit before thee: for, they are men wondered at: for, behold, I will bring forth my servant the BRANCH. For behold the stone that I have laid before Joshua; upon one stone shall be seven eyes: behold, I will engrave the graving thereof, saith the LORD of hosts, and I will remove the iniquity of that land in one day. In that day, saith the LORD of hosts, shall ye call every man his neighbour under the vine and under the fig tree" (Zechariah 3:1–10).

God promised to restore His people and make them His own. They were to be a royal, priestly and holy people in the middle of the earth: *"Now therefore, if ye will obey my voice indeed, and keep my covenant, then ye shall be a peculiar treasure unto me above all people: for all the earth is mine, And ye shall be unto me a kingdom of priests, and an holy nation. These are the words which thou shalt speak unto the children of Israel"* (Exodus 19:5–6; also compare to Isaiah 1:26–27). That is exactly what was said to Joshua the high priest, as the representative of his people (verses 6–7). According to verses 1 and 2, Joshua was compared to Jerusalem. Israel is prophesied to be the royal people in the coming Messianic kingdom. The third chapter of Zechariah describes how this new reinstatement will come about.

Revealed: Israel's True Enemy

"And he shewed me Joshua the high priest stand-ing before the angel of the LORD, and Satan standing at his right hand to resist him. And the LORD said unto Satan, The LORD rebuke thee, O Satan; even the LORD that hath chosen Jerusalem rebuke thee: is not this a brand plucked out of the fire?" (Zechariah 3:1–2). We've already mentioned that Satan is God's greatest enemy in spiritual history. He would like nothing more than to prevent Israel's reinstatement and the coming Messianic kingdom. God wants to heal and save; Satan wants to injure and destroy. It is the latter who continually accuses and persecutes Israel, as well as the Church of Jesus Christ. Scripture refers to Satan as the *"...god of this world"* who works in *"children of unbelief."* He brings the nations under his control to prevent God's work in Israel and the Church. His goal is to destroy Israel.

When the Lord said that Israel was like a brand plucked out of the fire, we see a glimpse of the long pe-riods of suffering God's people have experienced. Even in ancient Egypt, the Lord saved His people like a brand out of the fire. In the same way, He also saved them out of the four world Empires. Later, after their dispersion, God saved them from innumerable pogroms and inquisitions, and not least out of the fires of the Holocaust.

Psalm 66:12 refers to such times of suffering and

salvation through the Lord: *"Thou hast caused men to ride over our heads; we went through fire and through water: but thou broughtest us out into a wealthy place."* Isaiah 43:2 adds: *"When thou passest through the waters, I will be with thee; and through the rivers, they shall not overflow thee: when thou walkest through the fire, thou shalt not be burned; neither shall the flame kindle upon thee."*

At the end of time, another mighty confrontation will take place between the Lord and the dragon (Satan), and will result in Satan's being cast to the earth. Immediately he will begin to persecute Israel (Revelation 12:7–17), but the Lord will intervene at just the right moment and will pluck Israel like a brand out of the fire of destruction. Finally, He will bring His covenantal people to salvation, peace and rest. In this battle, which is prophetically foreshadowed in the book of Zechariah, salvation does come: *"And I heard a loud voice saying in heaven, Now is come salvation, and strength, and the kingdom of our God, and the power of his Christ: for the accuser of our brethren is cast down, which accused them before our God day and night"* (Revelation 12:10). The media and politicians continually accuse Israel because Satan uses the world as a weapon against God's people. How many United Nations resolutions have been directed against Israel and have led to her condemnation? Arab nations are among the Jews' most ardent accusers. The Jews were blamed and condemned for all sorts of things during the Nazi Reich. The Jews were libeled and condemned as guilty of ritual murder and well-poisoning during the Middle Ages. The nations didn't realize that they were being used as tools in Satan's hands.

Satan is also an enemy of the Church of Jesus Christ. Christians are continually accused of hypocrisy; they are humiliated, reviled, and in many parts of the world, they are even persecuted and killed.

Often we hear the accusers' voices, even within our own hearts: "Christians are no better than the others." That may be true, but we certainly do possess something better! We often fail to come up with a valid reason to be discontent with our own lives. But is it not written, *"Who shall lay any thing to the charge of God's elect? It is God that justifieth. Who is he that condemneth? It is Christ that died, yea rather, that is risen again, who is even at the right hand of God, who also maketh intercession for us,"* (Romans 8:33–34)? We don't stand before God clothed in our own righteousness, but in the righteousness of Jesus Christ.

How can we confront and dispel the enemy's accusations against us?

We cannot overcome his accusations through ignorance or desperation. However, it is written: *"And they overcame him by the blood of the Lamb, and by the word of their testimony; and they loved not their lives unto the death"* (Revelation 12:11). We overcome every type of accusation the enemy tries to use against us in the following ways:

- Through the blood of Christ for forgiveness
- Through the Word of God, and His promises
- By consciously placing our lives in Jesus' hands

We must learn to allow the Lord to speak for us. When the enemy accuses, we must admit our failure while clinging to God's promises: "Yes, I have sinned, I have failed, but I have humbled myself and have received forgiveness through the blood of the Lord Jesus. He is my High Priest!"

Israel's Own Unrighteousness

Apparently, Satan had good reason to accuse Joshua and Jerusalem, because the high priest was indeed clothed in filthy garments. This unrighteousness is Israel's own righteousness. The Bible says: *"But we are all as an unclean thing, and all our righteousnesses are as filthy rags; and we all do fade as a leaf; and our iniquities, like the wind, have taken us away"* (Isaiah 64:6). Israel will remain accused by the world for as long as she decides not to clothe herself with the righteousness of Christ.

Joshua remained the high priest despite his filthy garments. Why? Because God's gifts and calling are without repentance (Romans 11:29).

The Guarantee Of Israel's Restoration

"And he answered and spake unto those that stood

before him, saying, Take away the filthy garments from him. And unto him he said, Behold, I have caused thine iniquity to pass from thee, and I will clothe thee with change of raiment. And I said, Let them set a fair mitre upon his head. So they set a fair mitre upon his head, and clothed him with garments. And the angel of the LORD stood by" (Zechariah 3:4–5). The guarantee of Israel's restoration lies in the work of Christ. Joshua wasn't pardoned by the Lord because the accusations against him weren't justified, but because of God's mercy and love.

Three components make up Israel's future salvation, and serve as assurance for New Covenant believers. They speak louder than any accusation every could:

1. Her Election

"And the LORD said unto Satan, The LORD rebuke thee, O Satan; even the LORD that hath chosen Jerusalem rebuke thee" (Zechariah 3:2). God's sovereign election is much stronger than all of Satan's accusations. God's selection of a person takes place independently of any natural advantages or human efforts. Israel is called the "smallest" nation and is described as stiff-necked and stubborn (Deuteronomy 7:7 and 9:6), yet the Lord chose her: *"For thou art an holy people unto the LORD thy God, and the LORD hath chosen thee to be a peculiar people unto himself,*

above all the nations that are upon the earth" (Deuteronomy 14:2).

The Jews aren't holy on account of their own righteousness, but because of God's election. As a sign of this, Joshua had a *"fair mitre,"* or "clean turban," as rendered in the NIV, set upon his head (verse 5). Romans 11:28–29 explains just how far this election goes: *"As concerning the gospel, they are enemies for your sakes: but as touching the election, they are beloved for the fathers' sakes. For the gifts and calling of God are without repentance."* In this passage, Israel is called an "enemy" of the Gospel, yet, even that doesn't deter God from holding on to His chosen people.

All of Satan's attacks against Israel will ultimately fail on account of her divine election. This also applies to the true Church of Jesus Christ, which is made up exclusively of born-again believers. Let's re-read Romans 8:33: *"Who shall lay any thing to the charge of God's elect? It is God that justifieth."*

But we also read something else which reminds us of Joshua the priest: *"But ye are a chosen generation, a royal priesthood, an holy nation, a peculiar people; that ye should shew forth the praises of him who hath called you out of darkness into his marvellous light"* (1st Peter 2:9). Election is based solely upon a divine decision, and is absolutely independent of all human effort. When Satan attacks your election, he is really fighting against God's holy will, and for that reason he will never win.

However, in order that we not rest upon our election, we are called to work on it and make it sure: *"Wherefore the rather, brethren, give diligence to make your calling and election sure: for if ye do these things, ye shall never fall: For so an entrance shall be ministered unto you abundantly into the everlasting kingdom of our Lord and Saviour Jesus Christ"* (2nd Peter 1:10–11).

2. The Brand Out Of The Fire

"Is not this a brand plucked out of the fire?" (Zechariah 3:2). Fire is a picture of judgment (Matthew 3:11–12). All that has been plucked out of a fire has been saved from judgment. Where and how will Israel – and every other person – be plucked from out of the fire of judgment? At Calvary's Cross, where Jesus died a substitutional death for us! The fire of divine judgment was executed on the Cross of Calvary, on Him who hung on it so that we could be plucked from this judgment. This has already taken place for the Church of Jesus Christ, and will be fulfilled for Israel in the future.

As He hung on the Cross, Jesus said two things that point to the fire of divine judgment that He bore: *"After this, Jesus knowing that all things were now accomplished, that the scripture might be fulfilled, saith,*

I thirst" (John 19:28). Psalm 22:15 says: *"My strength is dried up like a potsherd; and my tongue cleaveth to my jaws; and thou hast brought me into the dust of death"* (Psalm 22:15). Jesus' substitutionary death plucked us out like a brand out of the fire of divine judgment: Those who believe will not be judged, but those who do not believe are already judged (John 3:18). Those who believe on Him have passed from death to life (John 5:24). God's wrath remains on those who do not believe: God is a consuming fire (Deuteronomy 4:24).

The blood of Christ, shed for our salvation, speaks louder than all accusations. Just as the blood of Abel cried accusingly to heaven (compare Genesis 4:10), the blood of Jesus Christ speaks much louder: *"And to Jesus the mediator of the new covenant, and to the blood of sprinkling, that speaketh better things than that of Abel"* (Hebrews 12:24). The accuser has to shout, but Jesus only needs to speak. Israel will also experience this forgiveness: *"Behold, I have caused thine iniquity to pass from thee, and I will clothe thee with change of raiment"* (Zechariah 3:4b). *"For behold the stone that I have laid before Joshua; upon one stone shall be seven eyes: behold, I will engrave the graving thereof, saith the LORD of hosts, and I will remove the iniquity of that land in one day"* (verse 9).

3. Jesus Stands By Joshua

"And I said, Let them set a fair mitre upon his

head. *So they set a fair mitre upon his head, and clothed him with garments. And the angel of the LORD stood by"* (Zechariah 3:5). Jesus (the angel of the Lord) is the guarantee for the righteousness and holiness of Israel and the Church. The high priest's mitre signifies holiness ("holiness to the Lord") and the clean garments signify righteousness. Both can only be attained through Jesus Christ.

When the prodigal son returned home, the father commanded: *"...Bring forth the best robe, and put it on him"* (Luke 15:22). The day will come when Isaiah 61:10 will be fulfilled: *"I will greatly rejoice in the LORD, my soul shall be joyful in my God; for he hath clothed me with the garments of salvation, he hath covered me with the robe of righteousness, as a bridegroom decketh himself with ornaments, and as a bride adorneth herself with her jewels."* We also can find peace in the One who ascended to the right hand of God and represents us before the Father. No accusation can ever take us away from God when Jesus is our personal Advocate.

The guarantee of Israel's future lies in the person of Jesus: *"Hear now, O Joshua the high priest, thou, and thy fellows that sit before thee: for they are men wondered at: for, behold, I will bring forth my servant the BRANCH. For behold the stone that I have laid before Joshua; upon one stone shall be seven eyes: behold, I will engrave the graving thereof, saith the*

LORD *of hosts, and I will remove the iniquity of that land in one day"* (Zechariah 3:8–9). *"Thus saith the LORD of hosts; If it be marvellous in the eyes of the remnant of this people in these days, should it also be marvellous in mine eyes? saith the LORD of hosts"* (Zechariah 8:6). The Jews are marvelous people because they have a marvelous God. God alone can perform miracles, and we all know that Israel's history is filled with them.

You are also a "marvelous" child of God, and the Church is a "marvelous" Church. I am reminded of an event recorded in Judges 13:18–19: *"And the angel of the LORD said unto him, Why askest thou thus after my name, seeing it is secret? So Manoah took a kid with a meat offering, and offered it upon a rock unto the LORD: and the angel did wonderously; and Manoah and his wife looked on."* According to Isaiah 9:6, Jesus is also called *"Wonderful, Counsellor."* Our God does wonders in every respect. And we, His people, can only stand and gaze in amazement! The wonder of Israel lies in the Servant, the Branch, and the Stone with seven eyes.

Jesus is the Servant of God who did the will of the Father. He humbled Himself and became a servant and even bore His Cross Himself. Isaiah described Him as follows: *"Behold my servant, whom I uphold; mine elect, in whom my soul delighteth; I have put my spirit upon him: he shall bring forth judgment to the Gen-*

tiles. *He shall not cry, nor lift up, nor cause his voice to be heard in the street. A bruised reed shall he not break, and the smoking flax shall he not quench: he shall bring forth judgment unto truth. He shall not fail nor be discouraged, till he have set judgment in the earth· and the isles shall wait for his law"* (Isaiah 42:1–4).

Jesus is the Branch of the Lord. The Branch from the house of David will set up the kingdom again (Isaiah 11:1). Israel will bear fruit in and through Him: *"In that day shall the branch of the LORD be beautiful and glorious, and the fruit of the earth shall be excellent and comely for them that are escaped of Israel. And it shall come to pass, that he that is left in Zion, and he that remaineth in Jerusalem, shall be called holy, even every one that is written among the living in Jerusalem"* (Isaiah 4:2–3; compare also to Isaiah 53:2).

Jesus is also the Stone that the builders rejected at that time. This Stone has become the cornerstone (Psalm 118:22). This cornerstone will also become Israel's ultimate salvation. The immovable foundation of our redemption was laid at Calvary: *"...upon this rock I will build my church"* (Matthew 16:18). Further, we read, *"Behold, I lay in Sion a chief corner stone, elect, precious: and he that believeth on him shall not be confounded"* (1st Peter 2:6). Jesus is also the Stone recorded in Daniel 2 which will come from heaven to earth at the end of the days. It will crush empires and become a mountain which fills the entire world. Jesus is also the headstone of Israel's salvation: *"Who art thou, O great mountain? before Zerubbabel thou shalt become a plain: and he shall bring forth the headstone thereof with shoutings, crying, Grace, grace unto it"* (Zechariah 4:7).

This Stone has seven eyes: *"For behold the stone that I have laid before Joshua; upon one stone shall be seven eyes"* (verse 9). These seven eyes point to the Lord's omnipotence, omniscience and divinity. Nothing is hidden from Him: *"And I beheld, and, lo, in the midst of the throne and of the four beasts, and in the midst of the elders, stood a Lamb as it had been slain, having seven horns and seven eyes, which are the seven Spirits of God sent forth into all the earth"* (Revelation 5:6; compare also with 1:4, 3:1 and 4:5). The fullness of the Spirit of God lives in Jesus. We have already seen that He sees the whole world and how the nations behave toward Israel: *"And they answered the angel of the LORD that stood among the myrtle trees, and said, We have walked to and fro through the earth, and, behold, all the earth sitteth still, and is at rest"* (Zechariah 1:11). But we also read in the letter to the Hebrews: *"Neither is there any creature that is not manifest in his sight: but all things are naked and opened unto the eyes of him with whom we have to do"* (Hebrews 4:13).

The passage concerning Israel's restoration as the royal nation among the nations closes with the words: *"I will remove the iniquity of that land in one day. In that day, saith the LORD of hosts, shall ye call every man his neighbour under the vine and under the fig tree"* (Zechariah 3:9b–10). On the day of Jesus' return, all of these prophecies will become reality in one single day (Isaiah 66:8). Then Israel will shine as the *"vine"* and Jerusalem as the *"fig tree"* in the millennial kingdom of Jesus Christ!

CHAPTER 6

THE FUTURE IS IN THE MESSIAH

"And the angel that talked with me came again, and waked me, as a man that is wakened out of his sleep, And said unto me, What seest thou? And I said, I have looked, and behold a candlestick all of gold, with a bowl upon the top of it, and his seven lamps thereon, and seven pipes to the seven lamps, which are upon the top thereof: And two olive trees by it, one upon the right side of the bowl, and the other upon the left side thereof. So I answered and spake to the angel that talked with me, saying, What are these, my lord? Then the angel that talked with me answered and said unto me, Knowest thou not what these be? And I said, No, my lord. Then he answered and spake unto me, saying, This is the word of the LORD unto Zerubbabel, saying, Not by might, nor by power, but by my spirit, saith the LORD of hosts. Who art thou, O great mountain? before Zerubbabel thou shalt become a plain: and he shall bring forth the headstone there-

of with shoutings, crying, Grace, grace unto it. Moreover the word of the LORD came unto me, saying, The hands of Zerubbabel have laid the foundation of this house; his hands shall also finish it; and thou shalt know that the LORD of hosts hath sent me unto you. For who hath despised the day of small things? for they shall rejoice, and shall see the plummet in the hand of Zerubbabel with those seven; they are the eyes of the LORD, which run to and fro through the whole earth" (Zechariah 4:1–10).

Israel is building a state in our day based on the strength of politics, negotiations and military power. However, Zechariah 4 explains that these things will not lead to the goal: *"Not by might, nor by power, but by my spirit, saith the LORD of hosts"* (verse 6). In this chapter, God reveals how this will all take place.

Israel bears witness to Bible prophecy fulfillment. When the Jewish state was founded in 1948, it instituted the golden candlestick with an olive branch on either side as its state emblem. Significant is that the great seven-armed candlestick (the menorah) — engraved with the words of Zechariah 4:16 — stands in front of the Knesset, the political parliament and seat of Israel's government. This is an unconscious, but prophetic sign that Israel is being drawn nearer to the fulfillment of the last of biblical prophecies. We are living in the days before Jesus' return! The very founding of the state of Israel is in accordance with Zechariah's endtime vision in chapter four.

1. Israel's Help

"*And the angel that talked with me came again, and waked me, as a man that is wakened out of his sleep, And said unto me, What seest thou? And I said, I have looked, and behold a candlestick all of gold, with a bowl upon the top of it, and his seven lamps thereon, and seven pipes to the seven lamps, which are upon the top thereof: And two olive trees by it, one upon the right side of the bowl, and the other upon the left side thereof. So I answered and spake to the angel that talked with me, saying, What are these, my lord? Then the angel that talked with me answered and said unto me, Knowest thou not what these be? And I said, No, my lord. Then he answered and spake unto me, saying, This is the word of the LORD unto Zerubbabel, saying, Not by might, nor by power, but by my spirit, saith the LORD of hosts*" (Zechariah 4:1–6). While Israel's "eyes" are only directed on politics, power and her armed forces at this moment, the eyes of the Lord of hosts are only focused on the Messiah. The Jews' longed-for salvation is only found in Him and His return. Israel's future, her righteousness, the millennium of peace under the lordship of the Messiah, the new, final Temple, and peace with the nations can never come about by military force, but only through His Spirit.

We must never lose sight of prophecy and Jesus' return. Verse 1 seems to draw our attention to this: *"And the angel that talked with me came again, and waked me, as a man that is wakened out of his sleep."* I believe that God wants to wake us out of our sleep. Just as the disciples fell asleep in the Garden of Gethsemane before the great hour of redemption, we, too, are in danger of falling asleep today.

Zechariah was awakened and his eyes were directed to the brightly shining candlestick (verse 2). This reminds us of the words of the Apostle Paul: *"And that, knowing the time, that now it is high time to awake out of sleep: for now is our salvation nearer than when we believed. The night is far spent, the day is at hand: let us therefore cast off the works of darkness, and let us put on the armour of light"* (Romans 13:11–12). The Lord spoke of the urgency of staying awake and keeping watch!

Consider the angel's question: *"What seest thou?"* (Zechariah 4:2). When God awakens us, He immediately draws our attention to the candlestick, which symbolizes the Lord. Spiritual awakening or revival means being given a new vision. Later on, the candlestick for the tabernacle had to be constructed and lit in such a way that each lamp illuminated the space in front of it (Exodus 25:37). The light was meant not only to illuminate the room, but also to be seen. The fullness of God's light falls upon the Lord, who fulfills the divine testimony, *"...in thy light shall we see light"* (Psalm 36:9).

Israel will be awakened and revived, and her eyes will be directed upon the Messiah during her darkest hour: The Great Tribulation. The two witnesses in Revelation 11, who are foreshadowed in Zechariah 4:14, will be responsible for this: *"I have looked, and behold a candlestick all of gold"* (verse 2). Revelation 1:12–14 says, *"And I turned to see the voice that spake with me. And being turned, I saw seven golden candlesticks; And in the midst of the seven candlesticks one like unto the Son of man, clothed with a garment down to the foot, and girt about the paps with a golden girdle. His head and his hairs were white like wool, as white as snow; and his eyes were as a flame of fire"* (Revelation 1:12–14).

As we've seen, the golden candlestick is a picture of the Lord Jesus and His working on behalf of Israel. He is the light of the world: *"I am the light of the world: he that followeth me shall not walk in darkness, but shall have the light of life"* (John 8:12). The gold points to the Lord's pure divinity. The Wise Men from the East honored Him with gold, frankincense and myrrh, and they worshipped Him shortly after His birth (Matthew 2:11).

The menorah had seven arms. The seven lamps that decorate the menorah symbolize the fullness of Jesus. The significance of the candlestick is personified in Isaiah 11:2 and we recognize the Lord Jesus Christ in it: *"And the spirit of the LORD shall rest upon him, the spirit of wisdom and understanding, the spirit of counsel and might, the spirit of knowledge and of the fear of the LORD."*

The main stem in the middle of the candlestick represents the Spirit of the Lord. Two arms come out of this, joined by the word "and":

- *"...the spirit of wisdom and understanding..."*
- *"...the spirit of counsel and might..."*
- *"...the spirit of knowledge and the fear of the LORD."*

Verse 10 points to the power of the Spirit of Jesus: *"They are the eyes of the Lord, which run to and fro through the whole earth."* Revelation 5:6 says: *"And I beheld, and, lo, in the midst of the throne and of the four beasts, and in the midst of the elders, stood a Lamb as it had been slain, having seven horns and seven eyes, which are the seven Spirits of God sent forth into all the earth."* Nothing escapes the Lord's bright, divine light. Zechariah 1:11 and 3:9 already see this number of the Spirit of Jesus.

The Lord Himself said, *"And the Father himself, which hath sent me, hath borne witness of me. Ye have neither heard his voice at any time, nor seen his shape. And ye have not his word abiding in you: for whom he hath sent, him ye believe not"* (John 5:37–38).

The two olive branches on either side of the candlestick (verse 3) represent Zerubbabel, the governor, and Joshua, the high priest. They are directly connected with the middle candlestick. Zerubbabel was mainly responsible for the return of the Jews from their Babylonian captivity, for the rebuilding of the Temple and for the reestablishment of Temple worship (see Ezra, Nehemiah and I Haggai). He was a direct descendant of David and a grandson of the Jewish king Jehoiachin, the last king of Judah (Matthew 12). Zerubbabel represented the kingdom of Israel; Joshua, as the high priest, represented Israel's priesthood (Zechariah 3).

Zerubbabel and Joshua were anointed with holy oil (verse 14). This is the only way they could be associated with the candlestick. Their two offices of king and priest are both united and fulfilled in Jesus Christ. The two olive branches beside the candlestick have a three-fold prophetic significance:

1. During Zechariah's time, they represented Zerubbabel and Joshua.

2. Presently, they refer to the Church, which is comprised of kings and priests (Revelation 1:6). Perhaps we can also see Israel and the Church in them, however, because Israel, though unconsciously, is still God's earthly witness.

3. In the future, they point to the two witnesses of whom it is said: *"And I will give power unto my two witnesses, and they shall prophesy a thousand two hundred and threescore days, clothed in sack-*

cloth. These are the two olive trees, and the two candlesticks standing before the God of the earth" (Revelation 11:3–4).

Israel's politics are destined to fail. Why? Because of the words: *"Not by might, nor by power, but by my spirit."* They will only succeed through Israel's Messiah, the Lord Jesus Christ.

C H A P T E R   7

THE JUDGMENTS BEFORE
JESUS RETURNS

"Then I turned, and lifted up mine eyes, and looked, and behold a flying roll (or scroll — NIV). And he said unto me, What seest thou? And I answered, I see a flying roll; the length thereof is twenty cubits, and the breadth thereof ten cubits. Then said he unto me, This is the curse that goeth forth over the face of the whole earth: for every one that stealeth shall be cut off as on this side according to it; and every one that sweareth shall be cut off as on that side according to it. I will bring it forth, saith the LORD of hosts, and it shall enter into the house of the thief, and into the house of him that sweareth falsely by my name: and it shall remain in the midst of his house, and shall consume it with the timber thereof and the stones thereof. Then the angel that talked with me went forth, and said unto me, Lift up now thine eyes, and see what is this that goeth forth. And I said, What

is it? And he said, This is an ephah that goeth forth. He said moreover, This is their resemblance through all the earth (verses 1–6). And, behold, there was lifted up a talent of lead: and this is a woman that sitteth in the midst of the ephah. And he said, This is wickedness. And he cast it into the midst of the ephah; and he cast the weight of lead upon the mouth thereof. Then lifted I up mine eyes, and looked, and, behold, there came out two women, and the wind was in their wings; for they had wings like the wings of a stork: and they lifted up the ephah between the earth and the heaven. Then said I to the angel that talked with me, Whither do these bear the ephah? And he said unto me, To build it an house in the land of Shinar: and it shall be established, and set there upon her own base. And I turned, and lifted up mine eyes, and looked, and, behold, there came four chariots out from between two mountains; and the mountains were mountains of brass. In the first chariot were red horses; and in the second chariot black horses; And in the third chariot white horses; and in the fourth chariot grisled and bay horses. Then I answered and said unto the angel that talked with me, What are these, my lord? And the angel answered and said unto me, These are the four spirits of the heavens, which go forth from standing before the Lord of all the earth. The black horses which are therein go forth into the north country; and the white *go forth after them; and the grisled go forth toward the south country. And the bay went forth, and sought to go that they might walk to and fro through the earth: and he said, Get you hence, walk to and fro through the earth. So they walked to and fro through the earth. Then cried he upon me, and spake unto me, saying, Behold, these that go toward the north country have quieted my spirit in the north country"* (Zechariah 5:1–6:8).

Zechariah's first five visions were encouraging ones of hope for the future of the Messianic kingdom. The next three visions concern the judgments that will come upon Israel and the world before Jesus returns in glory. Sin must be judged and removed before the Lord of hosts, who is also described as *"...the Lord of all the earth"* (chapter 6:5), returns. A kingdom of God cannot exist without justice. The Lord will take up His reign with an iron scepter. Revelation 12 and Isaiah 9 both allude to this: *"And she brought forth a man child, who was to rule all nations with a rod of iron: and her child was caught up unto God, and to his throne"* (Revelation 12:5). *"Of the increase of his government and peace there shall be no end, upon the throne of David, and upon his kingdom, to order it, and to establish it with judgment and with justice from henceforth even for ever. The zeal of the LORD of hosts will perform this"* (Isaiah 9:7).

1. The Flying Scroll And The Sins Of The Individual

"Then I turned, and lifted up mine eyes, and looked, and behold a flying roll. And he said unto me, What seest thou? And I answered, I see a flying roll; the length thereof is twenty cubits, and the breadth thereof ten cubits. Then said he unto me, This is the curse that goeth forth over the face of the whole earth: for every one that stealeth shall be cut off as on this side according to it; and every one that sweareth shall be cut off as on that side according to it. I will bring it forth, saith the LORD of hosts, and it shall enter into the house of the thief, and into the house of him that sweareth falsely by my name: and it shall remain in the midst of his house, and shall consume it with the timber thereof and the stones thereof" (Zechariah 5:1–4).

The first four verses of Zechariah make it clear that ultimately, every sin will be revealed before the un-bribable heavenly Judge.

Zechariah lifted up his eyes and saw (verse 1). We must also dare to lift up our eyes and see sin as God sees it. We live in a world where every sin and perversity is tolerated, or even worse, is made light of. The Word of God is no longer tolerated. However, man will not be asked for his opinion, about the time in which he lived, or about the prevailing trend of that day when he stands before the Judgment Seat of Christ. Instead, he will be asked whether or not he was obedient to God's Word. It is the only source that applies, which is why Zechariah saw a scroll that was so large that no human hand could hold it. This scroll symbolizes God's infallible Word (verse 2).

Since twenty cubits equal ten meters (34 feet), ten cubits would equal five. It is certainly no coincidence that the halls of Solomon's Temple, where the Law was read aloud, had the very same measurements as the scroll Zechariah saw: *"And the porch before the temple of the house, twenty cubits was the length thereof, according to the breadth of the house; and ten cubits was the breadth thereof before the house"* (1st Kings 6:3). The scroll was not rolled up, but was spread out so that it covered the porch of the Temple.

When God's judgments are poured out over the world, the Word of God will be unrolled, or opened, and will be the only measure by which the Lord will judge. Everything, including the judgments contained in the Holy Scriptures, will be fulfilled.

Let's recall how the Great Tribulation judgments begin: The Lamb of God will break the seven seals of the book (Revelation 5:5–7 and 6:1–onward), unleashing severe judgments upon this earth. We read: *"And I saw the dead, small and great, stand before God; and the books were opened: and another book was opened, which is the book of life: and the dead were judged out of those things which were written in the books, according to their works"* (Revelation 20:12).

Zechariah saw a flying scroll that united both heaven and earth; it was God's heavenly Word of judgment upon the earth. The flying scroll covered the entire land; nobody could escape it (verse 3). This judgment during the Great Tribulation will affect the land of Israel, but it will also come upon the nations.

The Word of God was sent for the salvation and forgiveness of all who believe it. However, for those who continually reject it and do not repent, it will become a curse and will lead to judgment: "*...with all deceivableness of unrighteousness in them that perish; because they received not the love of the truth, that they might be saved...That they all might be damned who believed not the truth, but had pleasure in unrighteousness*" (2nd Thessalonians 2:10,12). Those who do not believe the Gospel of Jesus Christ will be judged according to it: "*In the day when God shall judge the secrets of men by Jesus Christ according to my gospel*" (Romans 2:16).

Two terms that can be used to sum up the Ten Commandments written on the two stone tablets are used here: "*...every one that stealeth*" and "*...every one that swareth*" (Zechariah 5:3).

Taking advantage of our neighbors is classified as theft. But stealing God's glory, pursuing idols, or making a god of this world and all it offers are also considered theft. Even the selfish use of things God has given us, such as talents and material gifts, will be judged.

Lies that are taken so lightly today will also be judged relentlessly: *"But the fearful, and unbelieving, and the abominable, and murderers, and whoremongers, and sorcerers, and idolaters, and all liars, shall have their part in the lake which burneth with fire and brimstone: which is the second death...And there shall in no wise enter into it any thing that defileth, neither whatsoever worketh abomination, or maketh a lie: but they which are written in the Lamb's book of life"* (Revelation 21:8 and 27).

During the revelation of the Antichrist, who personifies lies, many people, including the Jews, will believe the lies, forsake God and deny Him, *"...Even him, whose coming is after the working of Satan with all power and signs and lying wonders"* (2nd Thessalonians 2:9).

People have gotten away with sinning for a long time, but time will soon run out. The day will come when all that is hidden will be revealed and judged by God. Those who do not believe in Jesus Christ will be condemned according to God's law: *"...Knowing this, that the law is not made for a righteous man, but for the lawless and disobedient, for the ungodly and for sinners, for unholy and profane, for murderers of fathers and murderers of mothers, for manslayers, For whoremongers, for them that defile themselves with mankind, for menstealers, for liars, for perjured persons, and if there be any other thing that is contrary to sound doctrine"* (1st Timothy 1:9–10).

No one will be spared from God's divine judgment, particularly during the Great Tribulation, but also, even now. It will arrive like an uninvited guest and will remain in the night of great distress. It will consume *"...the timber thereof and the stones thereof"* (verse 4). The Old Testament instructed that a house contaminated by leprosy should be destroyed in exactly the same way: *"And he shall break down the house, the stones of it, and the timber thereof, and all the morter of the house; and he shall carry them forth out of the city into an unclean place"* (Leviticus 14:45).

The Church is considered a house or temple, as is the individual believer. God will destroy anyone who defiles the Temple (1st Corinthians 3:16–17). That is why Ephesians 4:28 says: *"Let him that stole steal no more,"* and verse 25 says, *"Wherefore putting away lying, speak every man truth with his neighbour."* This is even more necessary because the time has come when judgment will begin at the house of God (1st Peter 4:17).

Surrendering our lives to Christ is the only way to avoid God's judgment. The forgiveness of sins and removal of the curse is only found in Christ. The balance of sin is immediately brought down to zero: *"For I will be merciful to their unrighteousness, and their sins and their iniquities will I remember no more"* (Hebrews 8:12).

2. The Ephah And The Sins Of The Nations

"Then the angel that talked with me went forth, and said unto me, Lift up now thine eyes, and see what is this that goeth forth. And I said, What is it? And he said, This is an ephah that goeth forth. He said moreover, This is their resemblance through all the earth. And, behold, there was lifted up a talent of lead: and this is a woman that sitteth in the midst of the ephah. And he said, This is wickedness. And he cast it into the midst of the ephah; and he cast the weight of lead upon the mouth thereof. Then lifted I up mine eyes, and looked, and, behold, there came out two women, and the wind was in their wings; for they had wings like the wings of a stork: and they lifted up the ephah between the earth and the heaven. Then said I to the angel that talked with me, Whither do these bear the ephah? And he said unto me, To build it an house in the land of Shinar: and it shall be established, and set there upon her own base" (Zechariah 5:5–11). God's future judgment will not only come upon the individual, or Israel, but upon the entire endtime Babylon. At that time, the ephah was the largest measurement for items such as grain. Zechariah explains that a woman called *"wickedness"* (verses 7–8) sat in this ephah. Subsequently, the godlessness of the endtime anti-Christian economy and politics is described.

The Jews returning to Israel from Babylon brought with them the heathen spirit of trade, which had no moral basis. Profit was more important than morals. God was not happy with that attitude, which is why these words are written in verse 6: *"This is their resemblance* (or iniquity — NIV) *through all the earth."* Since then, a large number of secular Jews have been involved in world trade. Godlessness in trade and economics has the political scene in its clutches today and contributes in almost unsurpassable measure to the corruption of the nations. It will reach its climax in endtime Babylon, and the road is being paved today. It was once very fittingly said, "It is not inflation that is destroying the nations, but godlessness, which is the cause of inflation." The concentration of evil will manifest itself in the endtimes, primarily in the economic sphere, drawing all mankind under its spell.

That is what the ephah symbolizes in verse 11 (see also Daniel 1:2). Zechariah describes two women as having wings like a stork (verse 9), a creature among the list of unclean beasts the Israelites were not permitted to eat. Leviticus 11:12,19 explain that the bird was considered an abomination (Leviticus 11:12 and 19).

The powers of uncleanness will promote the sins of anti-Christian Babylon. Endtime Babylon will become the earthly site of the revelation of the godless economy. However, the believing remnant of Israel should play no part in this anti-Christian Babylon, which is why a cover of lead is placed on the ephah (verse 8).

Revelation 17 and 18 refer to this endtime Babylon

as a "woman" or a "harlot." Revelation 17:1–5 and 18:4 explain that the Jews are to flee from this Babylon. The merchants of the earth will have become rich through the opulence of this Babylon. The entire Babylonian system will be destroyed in one hour (Revelation 18:3, 10 and onward).

We were given a foretaste of this time element on September 11th, 2001 when the World Trade Center was attacked. Both of the towers collapsed within the span of just one hour. The Antichrist will have such great power over the endtime economy that nobody will be able to buy or sell without him (Revelation 13:7). James offers a warning about this: *"Go to now, ye rich men, weep and howl for your miseries that shall come upon you. Your riches are corrupted, and your garments are motheaten. Your gold and silver is cankered; and the rust of them shall be a witness against you, and shall eat your flesh as it were fire. Ye have heaped treasure together for the last days"* (James 5:1–3).

3. The Apocalyptic Judgment Of The Endtimes

"And I turned, and lifted up mine eyes, and looked, and, behold, there came four chariots out from between two mountains; and the mountains were mountains of brass. In the first chariot were red horses; and in the second chariot black horses; And in the third chariot white horses; and in the fourth char-

iot grisled and bay horses. Then I answered and said unto the angel that talked with me, What are these, my lord? And the angel answered and said unto me, These are the four spirits of the heavens, which go forth from standing before the Lord of all the earth. The black horses which are therein go forth into the north country; and the white go forth after them; and the grisled go forth toward the south country. And the bay went forth, and sought to go that they might walk to and fro through the earth: and he said, Get you hence, walk to and fro through the earth. So they walked to and fro through the earth. Then cried he upon me, and spake unto me, saying, Behold, these that go toward the north country have quieted my spirit in the north country" (Zechariah 6:1–8).

Apocalyptic judgment is God's response to the increasing godlessness found in economics, politics and religion. The four chariots are drawn by different colored horses (verses 1–3). These chariots also represent spirits (verse 5). As they stand before the Lord, they are probably angels carrying out God's judgment on earth. Horses and chariots are often mentioned in the Bible in connection with power, war and judgment (compare Revelation 6, Jeremiah 46:9–10, Joel 2:3–11 and Nahum 3:1–7). The Lord's return is described in Revelation 19, where it is prophesied that He will come for judgment with His heavenly armies on horses to establish His kingdom (Revelation 19:11–16).

The angels of judgment written about in Zechariah 6 came from between two mountains (verse 1) which probably refer to Mount Zion and the Mount of Olives because they are directly connected with Jesus' return. The Valley of Jehoshaphat lies between the two mountains, which is also mentioned often in Scripture in connection with the Lord's judgment upon the nations (Joel 3:2).

The two mountains are described as brass, referring to a strength and stability which nothing can shake: *"And it shall come to pass in the last days, that the mountain of the Lord's house shall be established in the top of the mountains, and shall be exalted above the hills; and all nations shall flow unto it"* (Isaiah 2:2).

The chariots now go off for judgment in three separate directions:

- The black and white horses go north (verse 6).
- The grisled horses go south (verse 6).
- The strong, red horses go all over the earth (verse 7).

The horses are not limited to going in one direction. This picture fits the description of the judgments on the nations.

According to Daniel 11:40 and following, the kings of the North and South will arise to wage war against Israel.

The North refers to Babylon, which has always attacked Israel from that direction. It also refers to Assyria (Syria), which lies north of Israel. If we extend the definition of "north" a little farther, it stands for the power of Gog from the land of Magog in the far North (Ezekiel 38:1 — NIV). Ezekiel 38 and 39 explain that God will destroy this power. Micah 5:6 also says: *"And they shall waste the land of Assyria with the sword, and the land of Nimrod in the entrances thereof: thus shall he deliver us from the Assyrian, when he cometh into our land, and when he treadeth within our borders."*

The king of the South (Egypt) will be overcome and judged by the Lord (Daniel 11:42), which is summed up in Zechariah 10:11: *"...And the pride of Assyria shall be brought down, and the scepter of Egypt shall depart away."*

According to the book of Revelation, the apocalyptic judgments will come upon the entire world (verse 7). But only when the chariots go to the land of the north does the Spirit of God find rest (verse 8). Why? Because God's judgment upon the nations will end, and the Lord will return.

Therefore, the land of the North means "Babylon," which was the basis for a world-ruling power, the godless collaboration of the nations in rebellion against God (the Tower of Babel). Nimrod was the founder of Babylon (Genesis 10:8–10) and the first despot on earth. However, all the ungodly powers and the power of the last despot on earth will ultimately be united under the term "Babylon" (Revelation 17–18).

Israel was always attacked from the North by her enemies, even by the Romans. Therefore, verse 8 can be seen as a summary which says that judgment over all enemy nations opposing Israel and the Anointed (Psalm 2) have reached their ultimate fulfillment. Subsequently, the Lord's Spirit and jealousy for His people have been quieted.

The Lord said: *"I am jealous for Jerusalem and for Zion with a great jealousy. And I am very sore displeased with the heathen that are at ease"* in Zechariah 1:14–15. The Lord will appear in His glory now that judgment has been fulfilled and the Lord's Spirit and jealousy have been quieted. Israel will be led to rest in the kingdom of her Messiah, Jesus Christ: *"There remaineth therefore a rest to the people of God"* (Hebrews 4:9).

The nations will also enter into His rest: *"And in that day there shall be a root of Jesse, which shall stand for an ensign of the people; to it shall the Gentiles seek: and his rest shall be glorious"* (Isaiah 11:10).

Practically all of God's endtime judgments on earth are mentioned in Zechariah 5:1– 6:8:

- the judgment upon the people of the endtimes;
- the judgment upon endtime Babylon;
- the judgment upon the enemies from the north of Israel;
- the judgment upon the south; and
- the judgment upon the entire earth.

But, whoever believes on Jesus and gives his life to Him will not come into judgment! The Lord said this in John 5:24: *"Verily, verily, I say unto you, He that heareth my word, and believeth on him that sent me, hath everlasting life, and shall not come into condem-nation* (or judgment); *but is passed from death unto life."*

CHAPTER 8

THE DAWN OF A NEW DAY

"...And the word of the LORD came unto me, saying, Take of them of the captivity, even of Heldai, of Tobijah, and of Jedaiah, which are come from Babylon, and come thou the same day, and go into the house of Josiah the son of Zephaniah; Then take silver and gold, and make crowns, and set them upon the head of Joshua the son of Josedech, the high priest; And speak unto him, saying, Thus speaketh the LORD of hosts, saying, Behold the man whose name is The BRANCH; and he shall grow up out of his place, and he shall build the temple of the LORD: Even he shall build the temple of the LORD; and he shall bear the glory, and shall sit and rule upon his throne; and he shall be a priest upon his throne: and the counsel of peace shall be between them both. And the crowns shall be to Helem, and to Tobijah, and to Jedaiah, and to Hen the son of Zephaniah, for a memorial in the temple of the LORD. And they that

are far off shall come and build in the temple of the LORD, and ye shall know that the LORD of hosts hath sent me unto you. And this shall come to pass, if ye will diligently obey the voice of the LORD your God" (Zechariah 6:9–15).

The Man to whom spiritual history points is the Branch from the house of David. Everything will be laid before His feet. He will set up an unprecedented kingdom. The time is coming when Jesus will reign on earth as the King of Israel. The crowning of Joshua, the high priest, is symbolic of the crowning of the Messiah.

Zechariah was instructed to, *"Come thou the same day..."* (verse 2). In Israel, the day always begins in the evening. In other words, the new day begins with the night, which is described in chapters 5–6:8. Now, morning has come, the sun has risen, and with it something new has come.

This reminds us of the words from the prophet Isaiah: *"The burden of Dumah. He calleth to me out of Seir, Watchman, what of the night? Watchman, what of the night? The watchman said, The morning cometh, and also the night: if ye will enquire, enquire ye: return, come"* (Isaiah 21:11–12).

The day of the Lord will begin with the night of the Great Tribulation; the divine judgment of the world that leads to the new morning with Jesus' return and the establishment of the millennium of peace.

The Lord will return as the Sun of righteousness to end the night of the Great Tribulation. The Antichrist will meet divine judgment, but to Israel, the Lord promised: *"But unto you that fear my name shall the Sun of righteousness arise with healing in his wings; and ye shall go forth, and grow up as calves of the stall"* (Malachi 4:2).

When the Lord returns, His face will shine as the sun in its strength (Revelation 1:16). Jesus' Transfiguration was a foreshadow of this. There, too, His face shone like the sun: *"...his face did shine as the sun, and his raiment was white as the light"* (Matthew 17:2). Peter said this concerning the Lord's Transfiguration: *"...we made known unto you the power and coming of our Lord Jesus Christ...were eyewitnesses of his majesty"* (2nd Peter 1:16).

The sun is also a picture of the Messiah in Psalm 19:6, for none other than He is the Bridegroom: *"...as a bridegroom coming out of his chamber, and rejoiceth as a strong man to run a race."*

Israel's Coming New Day

Just as the early morning of Christ's resurrection brought in a completely new dispensation (Matthew 16:2), the early morning of Jesus' return will end the night and bring the dawn of the millennium of peace: *"For his anger endureth but a moment; in his favour is life: weeping may endure for a night, but joy cometh in the morning"* (Psalm 30:5). *"God is in the midst of her; she shall not be moved: God shall help her, and that right early"* (Psalm 46:5). Israel's believing remnant will be gathered to the Lord and will dedicate itself to Him.

Zechariah 6:10 refers to this prophetically: *"Take of them of the captivity, even of Heldai, of Tobijah, and of Jedaiah, which are come from Babylon, and come thou the same day, and go into the house of Josiah the son of Zephaniah."* These men represent the believing Jews when Jesus returns. They will have just returned from Babylon and brought an offering to rebuild the Temple. At Jesus' return, the Jews will be gathered from all parts of the world, and will be brought to Jerusalem: *"And he shall send his angels with a great sound of a trumpet, and they shall gather together his elect from the four winds, from one end of heaven to the other"* (Matthew 24:31).

God accepted the gifts from these men at that time and had a crown made for Joshua, the high priest. The Jews will be an offering to the Lord when they return at the *"...great sound of a trumpet."* And *"...I will set a sign among them, and I will send those that escape of them unto the nations, to Tarshish, Pul, and Lud, that draw the bow, to Tubal, and Javan, to the isles afar off, that have not heard my fame, neither have seen my glory; and they shall declare my glory among the Gentiles. And they shall bring all your brethren for an offering unto the LORD out of all nations upon horses, and in chariots, and in litters, and upon mules, and upon swift beasts, to my holy mountain Jerusalem, saith the LORD, as the children of Israel bring an offering in a clean vessel into the house of the LORD. And I will also take of them for priests and for Levites, saith the LORD"* (Isaiah 66:19–21).

Israel missed Jesus' birth in Bethlehem. The Wise Men from the East were the ones who had brought gifts to the Lord. Israel will not miss Christ's Second Coming. They will offer themselves to the Lord and recognize and receive Him as their King. The Jews who have returned from all over the world for their spiritual restoration will then be a crown of Jesus' triumph: *"Then take silver and gold, and make crowns, and set them upon the head of Joshua the son of Josedech, the high priest"* (Zechariah 6:11).

On one hand, Joshua (as we have already seen in chapter 3) represents the Jewish people (i.e. Jerusalem). The filthy garments are taken from him, he is clothed in fine robes, and a fair mitre is placed upon his head (chapter 3:4–5). The time is coming when both sorrow and suffering will be taken from Israel, and she will be crowned with the glory of the Messiah: *"...To appoint unto them that mourn in Zion, to give unto them beauty for ashes, the oil of joy for mourning, the garment of praise for the spirit of heaviness; that they might be called trees of righteousness, the planting of the LORD, that he might be glorified"* (Isaiah 61:3).

The Crowning Day

Joshua's crowning also represents the crowning of the Messiah Himself. He who once wore a crown of thorns because Israel rejected Him will, at her restoration, repentance and conversion, be made her King.

Psalm 8 is Messianic. Verse 5 says, *"For thou hast made him a little lower than the angels, and hast crowned him with glory and honour."* Isaiah 28:5 reads, *"In that day shall the LORD of hosts be for a crown of glory, and for a diadem of beauty, unto the residue of his people."*

This is why the statement concerning Joshua prophetically refers to the Messiah: *"...speak unto him, saying, Thus speaketh the LORD of hosts, saying, Behold the man whose name is The BRANCH...and he shall bear the glory, and shall sit and rule upon his throne; and he shall be a priest upon his throne: and the counsel of peace shall be between them both"* (Zechariah 6:12–13).

In chapter 3:8, the Lord is referred to as the *"BRANCH."* He will come for the *"...men wondered at"* — that is Israel. Consider these verses:

• Isaiah 11:1: *"And there shall come forth a rod out of the stem of Jesse, and a Branch shall grow out of his roots."*

• Jeremiah 23:5: *"Behold, the days come, saith the LORD, that I will raise unto David a righteous Branch, and a King shall reign and prosper, and shall execute judgment and justice in the earth."*

• Jeremiah 33:15: *"In those days, and at that time, will I cause the Branch of righteousness to grow up unto David; and he shall execute judgment and righteousness in the land."*

After the Lord Jesus was born and was later taken to Nazareth, He grew up there so that the prophet's statement would be fulfilled: *"He shall be called a Nazarene"* (Matthew 2:23). The name *"Nazareth"* comes from the word *netzer,* which means *"rod."* This statement probably refers to Isaiah 11:1. Matthew's Gospel account is the Gospel of the Jews.

The Coming Glory

When Jesus returns, He will build the Temple of the Lord, from which, according to Zechariah 14:8, living water will flow. The Dead Sea will be rejuvenated and the trees will bring forth fruit twelve times a year for the healing of the nations (Ezekiel 47:7–12 and Revelation 22:2). This must have been a wonderful message for the Jews of that time. They were building the second Temple, which was not comparable to the glory of the Temple Solomon had built. But they were encouraged through this promise that the Lord Himself would one day come to build His Temple and reign from Jerusalem. Although the Temple they were building was quite modest, their work was not in vain. Later, Jesus said that this was His Father's house.

Israel's sacrifices in the newly built Temple were accepted and prophetically pointed to the future. The people should not despise small things or small beginnings (chapter 4:10), for one day Haggai 2:9 would be fulfilled: *"The glory of this latter house shall be greater than of the former, saith the LORD of hosts: and in this place will I give peace, saith the LORD of hosts."*

Our Coming Reward

This is also how it is with our work. However trivial it may seem to us, the Lord sees it as valuable because it serves toward the building of the kingdom of Christ. One day we shall see the importance of every work, service and gift for Jesus. Then we shall see the importance of surrendering and dedicating ourselves completely to Him. For just as Joshua's crown was kept in the Temple as a memorial (verse 14), everything we do through the grace of the Holy Spirit will be kept as a memorial. Every gift serves the glory of the Lord and will one day be rewarded. This is why the Apostle Paul admonished and encouraged the Corinthians: *"...be ye stedfast, unmoveable, always abounding in the work of the Lord, forasmuch as ye know that your labour is not in vain in the Lord"* (1st Corinthians 15:58).

Strangers Will Be Included

The Lord's kingdom will be so glorious, and His praise will be spread over the earth so quickly, that even strangers from among the nations will come and take part in the building of the Temple: *"And they that are far off shall come and build in the temple of the LORD, and ye shall know that the LORD of hosts hath sent me unto you. And this shall come to pass, if ye will diligently obey the voice of the LORD your God"* (Zechariah 6:15).

Chapter 2:15 says that many from out of the nations will join themselves to the Lord and become His people. Isaiah 19 says that Egypt and Assyria (Syria) will also serve the Lord: They will be blessed, and, together with Israel, they will become a blessing on earth (Isaiah 19:23–25). Previously we read that judgment was proclaimed over Israel, but now, in the new morning, the sun will rise for them, too.

But other nations will also join themselves to the Lord: *"Also the sons of the stranger...will I bring to my holy mountain, and make them joyful in my house of prayer: their burnt offerings and their sacrifices shall be accepted upon mine altar; for mine house shall be called an house of prayer for all people"* (Isaiah 56:6–7), and, *"...the sons of strangers shall build up thy walls, and their kings shall minister unto thee: for in my wrath I smote thee, but in my favour have I had mercy on thee"* (Isaiah 60:10).

Israel In The New Day

Three times we read that Israel should know *"...that the Lord of hosts hath sent me unto you"* (Zechariah 6:15; also compare to 4:9 and 2:15). All things will culminate in the knowledge of Jesus, which produces life out of death.

If a lack of knowledge regarding the Messiah brought the Jewish people destruction —*"...my people are gone into captivity, because they have no knowledge"* (Isaiah 5:13) — then they will receive life in abundance when they recognize Jesus: *"They shall not hurt nor destroy in all my holy mountain: for the earth shall be full of the knowledge of the LORD, as the waters cover the sea"* (Isaiah 11:9). The same is said in Habakkuk 2:14: *"For the earth shall be filled with the knowledge of the glory of the LORD, as the waters cover the sea."*

It is of eternal significance for every person to know Jesus: *"And this is life eternal, that they might know thee the only true God, and Jesus Christ, whom thou hast sent"* (John 17:3). To know Him means to be convinced by the Holy Spirit and the Word of God that Jesus is the Redeemer, to acknowledge this and receive Him into your heart and life. Whoever does so will enter into the kingdom of God.

CHAPTER 9

A TERRIBLE AWAKENING

"And it came to pass in the fourth year of king Darius, that the word of the LORD came unto Zechariah in the fourth day of the ninth month, even in Chisleu; When they had sent unto the house of God Sherezer and Regemmelech, and their men, to pray before the LORD, And to speak unto the priests which were in the house of the LORD of hosts, and to the prophets, saying, Should I weep in the fifth month, separating myself, as I have done these so many years? Then came the word of the LORD of hosts unto me, saying, Speak unto all the people of the land, and to the priests, saying, When ye fasted and mourned in the fifth and seventh month, even those seventy years, did ye at all fast unto me, even to me? And when ye did eat, and when ye did drink, did not ye eat for yourselves, and drink for yourselves? Should ye not hear the words which the LORD hath cried by the former prophets, when Jerusalem was inhabited and in pros-

perity, and the cities thereof round about her, when men inhabited the south and the plain? And the word of the LORD came unto Zechariah, saying, Thus speaketh the LORD of hosts, saying, Execute true judgment, and shew mercy and compassions every man to his brother: And oppress not the widow, nor the fatherless, the stranger, nor the poor; and let none of you imagine evil against his brother in your heart. But they refused to hearken, and pulled away the shoulder, and stopped their ears, that they should not hear. Yea, they made their hearts as an adamant stone, lest they should hear the law, and the words which the LORD of hosts hath sent in his spirit by the former prophets: therefore came a great wrath from the LORD of hosts. Therefore it is come to pass, that as he cried, and they would not hear; so they cried, and I would not hear, saith the LORD of hosts: But I scattered them with a whirlwind among all the nations whom they knew not. Thus the land was desolate after them, that no man passed through nor returned: for they laid the pleasant land desolate" (Zechariah 7:1–14).

Imagine yourself in the following situation: You've planned a trip. You enter the train quite confidently, making yourself comfortable. You can already envision what your destination will look like when, suddenly, you notice that the train is traveling in the wrong direction!

There have been, and will be, moments in our lives when we suddenly realize that the things we were convinced were right, or that we've done for years, were actually wrong. It must have been a similar situation for the people Zechariah wrote about.

Their Sincere Endeavor

"And it came to pass in the fourth year of king Darius, that the word of the LORD came unto Zechariah in the fourth day of the ninth month, even in Chisleu; When they had sent unto the house of God Sherezer and Regemmelech, and their men, to pray before the LORD, And to speak unto the priests which were in the house of the LORD of hosts, and to the prophets, saying, Should I weep in the fifth month, separating myself, as I have done these so many years?" (Zechariah 7:1–3). Approximately two years after Zechariah had received the eight prophetic visions of Israel's future and the Messianic kingdom (compare chapter 1:7 with 7:1), a delegation from Bethel came to Jerusalem armed with an urgent question.

It is impressive that an entire community had a common religious cause, a question that concerned them. It was not a political question, but a religious one, that so troubled the inhabitants of Bethel that they sent a delegation to Jerusalem (verse 2). Bethel once had been the center of religious apostasy for the ten northern tribes of Israel by Jeroboam (1st Kings 12:26–33). But now men came from Bethel seeking the God of Israel. Wouldn't it be great if our towns and cities were moved by the search for God and the desire to please and serve Him? How wonderful it would be if our governors and mayors sought God and His will, and no journey would be too far, and no effort too great, to find the answer to this question! How incredible it would be if the question of true worship took up more of their time than political issues! The best politicians have always been those who sought first the kingdom of God. Joseph, Daniel, Mordecai, Esther, Ezra, Zerubbabel and many others are examples of leaders who were more concerned with seeking the Lord. What concerns our leaders now?

The authorities and other inhabitants of Bethel were asking whether they could stop fasting now that they had returned from their Babylonian captivity and the Temple had been rebuilt (verse 3). They didn't interrupt their fasting or just stop doing it; they wanted to know God's will and act accordingly. They really wanted to do what pleased God!

How many decisions do we make today without first consulting God? A phrase in our text particularly speaks of this: *"...to pray before the Lord"* (verse 2). Where does this take place today? This doesn't refer to the reading of a religious liturgy; it means really praying about something. To the Philippians, Paul wrote:

"Be careful for nothing; but in every thing by prayer and supplication with thanksgiving let your requests be made known unto God" (Philippians 4:6). Therefore, the delegation from Bethel first went to the Temple to seek the God of Israel and to pray (verse 2). Only after this did they go to the priests and prophets with their question. It seems as though a new spirit was placed in those who had returned from Babylon.

To a large extent, we have forgotten the importance of seeking God's will. Instead, we want to take things into our own hands. We have so many means at our disposal of reaching our goals that we think we can do so without the Lord.

The men from Bethel were concerned with the issue of fasting in the fifth month of the year (verse 3). The Jews had introduced a few fasts of their own that had not been expressly ordered by God. These fasts, including the ones in the fifth and seventh months (verse 5), were the way they chose to remember various events, such as Nebuchadnezzar's destruction of Jerusalem and the destruction of Solomon's Temple.

Another day of fasting in the seventh month was in remembrance of the murder of Jerusalem's governor Gedaliah. After Jerusalem had been conquered by Nebuchadnezzar and King Zedekiah had been taken captive, the Babylonian king made Gedaliah governor of Jerusalem (Jeremiah 40:5). Gedaliah was God-fearing and reliable, but unfortunately he was also very gullible. He was murdered by his own people in the seventh month of his rule (Jeremiah 41:1–2).

Now the Jews had returned from 70 years of Babylonian captivity. Jerusalem and the Temple had been rebuilt, and the time of grieving was over. So the question naturally arose: "Should we still fast over Jerusalem's destruction even though the Lord has brought us back and shown us new grace?" The delegation came to Jerusalem filled with a great desire to know God's will. They came to ask Him, and the whole city was behind them and this question.

The Insincerity Of Their Hearts

"Then came the word of the LORD of hosts unto me, saying, Speak unto all the people of the land, and to the priests, saying, When ye fasted and mourned in the fifth and seventh month, even those seventy years, did ye at all fast unto me, even to me? And when ye did eat, and when ye did drink, did not ye eat for yourselves, and drink for yourselves? Should ye not hear the words which the LORD hath cried by the former prophets, when Jerusalem was inhabited and in prosperity, and the cities thereof round about her, when men inhabited the south and the plain?" (Zechariah 7:4). Their expectation was surely great. God's answer must have been all the more alarming. They found out that God had looked upon their self-imposed fasts with different eyes: *"Did ye at all fast unto me?"* (verse

5). This counter-question must have come as a shocking revelation to them!

Is that which we do really for the Lord? Those people were convinced that they were doing the right thing, yet the Lord said that He could not accept it. They fasted twice a year; they prayed, lamented and wept, reminding themselves of the past— yet it was all in vain. The Lord did not accept their actions.

As we already mentioned, we can serve the Lord without following Him, but we cannot follow Him without serving Him. We can be religious, even to an extreme; we can keep self-imposed laws, but this doesn't bring us an inch closer to the Lord. For all service to God, even if it is of religious origin, is futile if it does not originate in the Holy Spirit.

All worship had become a mere form of religion, as the Lord Jesus said later on to the Church in Sardis: *"...thou hast a name that thou livest, and art dead"* (Revelation 3:1). Despite all their religious earnestness, Israel was still practicing meaningless formalities. Religious, ritual customs did not reflect an inner conversion to God.

Nothing can replace obedience to God's Word. Fulfilling religious duties out of habit can never replace the surrender of our hearts. The Lord made this quite clear when, one day, His relatives came to Him. They had sought Him and found Him, and His followers drew His attention to the fact that His relatives were there, but the Lord said, *"...Who is my mother, or my brethren? And he looked round about on them which sat about him, and said, Behold my mother and my brethren! For whosoever shall do the will of God, the same is my brother, and my sister, and mother"* (Mark 3:33–35).

On another occasion, the Lord Jesus said these well-known words: *"Not every one that saith unto me, Lord, Lord, shall enter into the kingdom of heaven; but he that doeth the will of my Father which is in heaven. Many will say to me in that day, Lord, Lord, have we not prophesied in thy name? and in thy name have cast out devils? and in thy name done many wonderful works? And then will I profess unto them, I never knew you: depart from me, ye that work iniquity"* (Matthew 7:21–23).

Obedience Is Better Than Sacrifice

Why were the Jews' prayers not heard when they fasted?

They Fasted For Selfish Reasons

"And when ye did eat, and when ye did drink, did not ye eat for yourselves, and drink for yourselves?" (Zechariah 7:6). Neither their fasting nor their celebrating were performed for the glory of the Lord. This is a convicting example of how deeply God can see into our hearts. "Religiosity" does not reach God or please Him because it is characterized by selfishness. This is

a religiosity where the Lord is not its goal. It doesn't serve the Lord's glory and honor; it serves our own selfishness. What have we turned religious celebrations such as Christmas and Easter into? We have made them into festivals of eating, drinking and entertainment instead of keeping them sacred for the Lord of Glory. Think of all the Sundays that have come and gone. Have we used them to seek fellowship with God or have we used them for our own purposes? We should examine ourselves before the Lord, asking ourselves the extent to which we really concerned with Him.

The Israelites fasted at that specific time every year for seventy years. But they weren't liberated because of their fasting, they were liberated because of Daniel's prayer of repentance and humility (Daniel 9).

They Did Something God Had Not Commanded

This self-imposed religious act was not in accordance with God's will: *"...lest they should hear the law, and the words which the LORD of hosts hath sent in his spirit by the former prophets"*(verse 12). A fleshly, emotional striving that does not come from the Spirit of God is futile. Many people believe they can please God when they do good things, or if they are religious. However, the Bible very clearly teaches that this is impossible. Every person remains unforgiven if he or she has not been born again. Only when we have been regenerated through the Holy Spirit by receiving Christ into our lives can we do the works that please God out of our new spiritual lives. This is why the Lord once said, *"...why call ye me, Lord, Lord, and do not the things which I say?"* (Luke 6:46).

The only thing that counts is whether or not a person believes in Christ: *"Then said they unto him, What shall we do, that we might work the works of God? Jesus answered and said unto them, This is the work of God, that ye believe on him whom he hath sent"* (John 6:28–29).

Their False Attitude Is Revealed
- They refused to listen
- They shrugged their shoulders
- They stopped their ears
- They hardened their hearts
- They didn't listen to the words of the Spirit (verses 11–12).

Many people persevere in their religious formalism. They are not prepared to open up to the Word of God and His will. There are people who believe in God and do many good works, but they do not want to know anything about Jesus. However, when a person continually turns away from God's will, he becomes more and more rejecting, harder and unresponsive to the truth. Jesus expressed this with the parable of the sower. When the seed of God's Word falls upon the downtrodden path, it is unable to penetrate the earth, and the wicked one comes along and takes it away: *"When any one heareth the word of the kingdom, and understandeth it not, then cometh the wicked one, and catcheth away that which was sown in his heart. This is he which received seed by the way side"* (Matthew 13:19).

Trodden-down paths, false attitudes and religious convictions are the greatest hindrance to the Gospel of Jesus Christ. We do not make any inner progress when we say: "That's how I've always been and that's how I am going to stay!" An unchangeable attitude such as this also brought great harm to the Jews: The destruction of the Temple and their dispersion among the nations. This was what happened in Old Testament times (before Babylon) and also after the rejection of Messiah, in 70 A.D. Since then, Israel has had no sacrifice, no priest and no temple. *"Therefore it is come to pass, that as he cried, and they would not hear; so they cried, and I would not hear, saith the LORD of hosts: But I scattered them with a whirlwind among all the nations whom they knew not. Thus the land was desolate after them, that no man passed through nor returned: for they laid the pleasant land desolate"* (Zechariah 7:13–14).

How Things Can Change

"Thus speaketh the LORD of hosts, saying, Exe-

cute true judgment, and shew mercy and compassions every man to his brother: And oppress not the widow, nor the fatherless, the stranger, nor the poor; and let none of you imagine evil against his brother in your heart" (Zechariah 7:9–10). These verses tell us to:

- Be honest, and consider the Word of God as the only guideline for yourself, your family and your state. Be faithful and reliable.
- Be ruled by kindness and mercy, not selfishness.
- Do good to others who are not as fortunate as you. Be aware of your neighbor's needs.
- Do not be envious, but respect one another.

This is all summarized by a statement made by James: *"Wherefore lay apart all filthiness and super-fluity of naughtiness, and receive with meekness the engrafted word, which is able to save your souls. But be ye doers of the word, and not hearers only, deceiving your own selves"* (James 1:21–22). Here, the proper sequence of how a person can please God is shown: 1) repent; 2) receive the Word of God; and 3) become a doer of the Word. We are told that everything else is self-deception. God only accepts us through His Son Jesus Christ.

Perhaps today you've noticed that you are sitting in the wrong train, a train that is headed in the wrong direction. Have you seen how your own efforts have gotten you nowhere? God is giving you the opportunity to change trains right now. There's still time. Take advantage of this opportunity. If you ask Him with a sincere heart, He can even restore lost years to you. Despite everything you've done until now, the Lord is asking for your heart.

CHAPTER 10

THE WORDS THAT DETERMINE
THE FUTURE

"Again the word of the LORD of hosts came to me, saying, Thus saith the LORD of hosts; I was jealous for Zion with great jealousy, and I was jealous for her with great fury. Thus saith the LORD; I am returned unto Zion, and will dwell in the midst of Jerusalem: and Jerusalem shall be called a city of truth; and the mountain of the LORD of hosts the holy mountain. Thus saith the LORD of hosts; There shall yet old men and old women dwell in the streets of Jerusalem, and every man with his staff in his hand for very age. And the streets of the city shall be full of boys and girls playing in the streets thereof. Thus saith the LORD of hosts; If it be marvellous in the eyes of the remnant of this people in these days, should it also be marvellous in mine eyes? saith the LORD of hosts. Thus saith the LORD of hosts; Behold, I will save my people from the east country, and from the west coun-

try; And I will bring them, and they shall dwell in the midst of Jerusalem: and they shall be my people, and I will be their God, in truth and in righteousness. Thus saith the LORD of hosts; Let your hands be strong, ye that hear in these days these words by the mouth of the prophets, which were in the day that the foundation of the house of the LORD of hosts was laid, that the temple might be built. For before these days there was no hire for man, nor any hire for beast; neither was there any peace to him that went out or came in because of the affliction: for I set all men every one against his neighbour. But now I will not be unto the residue of this people as in the former days, saith the LORD of hosts. For the seed shall be prosperous; the vine shall give her fruit, and the ground shall give her increase, and the heavens shall give their dew; and I will cause the remnant of this people to possess all these things. And it shall come to pass, that as ye were a curse among the heathen, O house of Judah, and house of Israel; so will I save you, and ye shall be a blessing: fear not, but let your hands be strong. For thus saith the LORD of hosts; As I thought to punish you, when your fathers provoked me to wrath, saith the LORD of hosts, and I repented not; So again have I thought in these days to do well unto Jerusalem and to the house of Judah: fear ye not. These are the things that ye shall do; Speak ye every man the truth to his neighbour; execute the judgment of truth and peace in *your gates: And let none of you imagine evil in your hearts against his neighbour; and love no false oath: for all these are things that I hate, saith the LORD. And the word of the LORD of hosts came unto me, saying, Thus saith the LORD of hosts; The fast of the fourth month, and the fast of the fifth, and the fast of the seventh, and the fast of the tenth, shall be to the house of Judah joy and gladness, and cheerful feasts; therefore love the truth and peace. Thus saith the LORD of hosts; It shall yet come to pass, that there shall come people, and the inhabitants of many cities: And the inhabitants of one city shall go to another, saying, Let us go speedily to pray before the LORD, and to seek the LORD of hosts: I will go also. Yea, many people and strong nations shall come to seek the LORD of hosts in Jerusalem, and to pray before the LORD. Thus saith the LORD of hosts; In those days it shall come to pass, that ten men shall take hold out of all languages of the nations, even shall take hold of the skirt of him that is a Jew, saying, We will go with you: for we have heard that God is with you"* (Zechariah 8:1–23).

After receiving such a strong warning in Zechariah 7, the Jews now found themselves on the receiving end of an encouraging message. Hosea wrote that the Lord tears, but He also heals, He smites, but He also binds up (Hosea 6:1). Sorrow will come to an end, and the time of fasting will become a time of joy (Zechariah 8:19). The Lord encouraged His people with the words, *"Let your hands be strong, ye that hear in these days these words by the mouth of the prophets, which were in the day that the foundation of the house of the LORD of hosts was laid, that the temple might be built"* (verse 9). Haggai and Zechariah are the two prophets mentioned. They were in Jerusalem when the building of the Temple began (Ezra 5:1). In verses 13 and 15 the Lord also said, *"Fear not, but let your hands be strong...fear ye not."*

Zechariah 7 ends with the words, *"...I scattered them with a whirlwind among all the nations whom they knew not. Thus the land was desolate after them, that no man passed through nor returned: for they laid the pleasant land desolate."* For the most part, this prophecy was fulfilled in 70 A.D.

Chapter 8 explains Israel's endtime gathering and restoration. The Lord gave this prophecy when the Jews had returned from Babylon, *"And I will bring them, and they shall dwell in the midst of Jerusalem: and they shall be my people, and I will be their God, in truth and in righteousness"* (verse 8).

We will discuss four main points in this chapter:
1. Who determines the future?
2. What purpose does the future serve?
3. What does the future hold?
4. What we can learn from history for the future?

Who Determines The Future?

Let's begin with a list of those who do not determine the future: The nations do not determine Jerusalem's future; nor do United Nations resolutions or sanctions; nor does the Islamic movement. Israel is not the victim of fate, rulings, victorious powers, or the ebb and flow of history—Israel's future is solely determined by God. *"Again the word of the LORD of hosts came to me, saying, Thus saith the LORD of hosts; I was jealous for Zion with great jealousy, and I was jealous for her with great fury"* (Zechariah 8:1–2). These two verses sound like words of thunder pealing out of eternity. They are words for Israel, but they are also words against the nations. One might even say they echo Zechariah 1:14–15: *" ...I am jealous for Jerusalem and for Zion with a great jealousy. And I am very sore displeased with the heathen that are at ease."* The Lord of hosts is speaking and it is His Word the prophet is given. This statement is repeated throughout chapter 8, in verses 1–4, 6–7, 9, 14, 17–20 and 23.

Israel's future is not based on human discovery any more than she is the product of human effort or coincidence. The return of the Jews to their homeland, the founding of the state of Israel in 1948, and the capture of Jerusalem in 1967 are proof of the power of God's Word. That the Jews are living in their land documents the truth and reliability of God's Word. Israel's past, present and future are under His Word and promises.

Those who have been born again by His Spirit are under God's immovable promises in Jesus Christ: *"But the word of the Lord endureth for ever. And this is the word which by the gospel is preached unto you"* (1st Peter 1:25). Israel is a nation of wonders because she has a wonderful God: *"Thus saith the LORD of hosts; If it be marvellous in the eyes of the remnant of this people in these days, should it also be marvellous in mine eyes? saith the LORD of hosts"* (Zechariah 8:6).

The Word of God surpasses all human comprehension. The Israelites probably couldn't grasp what was being said to them. But we know that all things are possible with God. He sends light in the deepest darkness. He led His people out of the Holocaust and back to their homeland. He gave them the greatest victories over their enemies, and He will also give them a future with the Messiah, which we read in Zechariah 3:8: *"Hear now, O Joshua the high priest, thou, and the fellows that sit before thee: for they are men wondered at: for, behold, I will bring forth my servant the BRANCH."*

Jesus Christ is the Branch. He is the Wonderful Counselor of Isaiah 9:5 Who came to Israel and Who will return there; Who did wonders and Who will do wonders again. Is anything too wonderful for Him (Genesis 18:14)? When Manoah, Samson's father, asked after the name of the Lord, He answered: *"Why do you ask my name, seeing it is wonderful?"* (Judges 13:18 — The Amplified Bible). This wonderful God will carry out Israel's future in a wondrous way!

Do we need proof of the power of God's Word? Here we have it! *"Thus saith the LORD of hosts; Behold, I will save my people from the east country, and from the west country; And I will bring them, and they shall dwell in the midst of Jerusalem: and they shall be my people, and I will be their God, in truth and in righteousness"* (Zechariah 8:7–8). The terms "east" and "west" country are probably symbolic for the entire world.

Israel's return from Babylon was unidirectional. Israel's return today is occurring from all directions. This is unprecedented and further proves the reliability of God's Word. Israel is being effectually led toward the Messiah. Nothing can prevent God from doing this; neither another Holocaust, nor any world power will be able to oppose His plans for His land and people.

Israel's return in our day is a foretaste of the complete fulfillment in the millennium of peace (verse 8). It's the fragrant "aroma" wafting from the kitchen before you sit down at the table to eat and enjoy a meal.

What Purpose Does The Future Serve?

The purpose of the future is to glorify the Lord. Zechariah 8:3 makes this clear: *"Thus saith the*

LORD; I am returned unto Zion, and will dwell in the midst of Jerusalem: and Jerusalem shall be called a city of truth: and the mountain of the LORD of hosts the holy mountain." Who is returning to Zion?

Israel's restoration serves the unique, exalted purpose that the Lord can return to establish His kingdom in, with, and through Israel. In Acts 15:15–16, James explains what is meant by this: *"And to this agree the words of the prophets; as it is written, After this I will return, and will build again the tabernacle of David, which is fallen down; and I will build again the ruins thereof, and I will set it up."*

Jesus is the God of Israel. He is bringing His people back to His land for one reason: To become their God visibly before the world: *"And I will bring them, and they shall dwell in the midst of Jerusalem: and they shall be my people, and I will be their God, in truth and in righteousness"* (Zechariah 8:8). The word "truth" is mentioned in verses 3 and 8, and both times it refers to God's truth. Jerusalem is called the "city of truth" because it reminds us of God's truth. It becomes visible in her that the Lord has fulfilled all of His promises. Then He will be her God *"...in truth and righteousness."* All the nations, particularly Israel, will be amazed.

Israel's Future Serves Two Purposes:
   1). Israel's Future Serves The Fulfillment Of God's

Promise To Abraham:

"And it shall come to pass, that as ye were a curse among the heathen, O house of Judah, and house of Israel: so will I save you, and ye shall be a blessing: fear not, but let your hands be strong" (Zechariah 8:13). God promised Abraham, *"...I will make of thee a great nation, and I will bless thee, and make thy name great; and thou shalt be a blessing"* (Genesis 12:2). God's covenant with Abraham rests on His free and sovereign promise (Genesis 12:1,3; 15:7–18 and 22:16–18). Moses made a covenant with the people in Deuteronomy 28:69 and spoke about the blessing they would receive in exchange for their obedience (verses 1–2 onward), but he also warned of the curse they would experience if they were disobedient (verse 15 onward). The curse Moses pronounced referred to the Sinai covenant God had made with His people. In Exodus 19:5–8, the people accepted God's covenant given through Moses. But it wasn't long before they disobeyed and were punished. But just as Moses' curse over Israel became real, so too, will God's promise to Abraham be fulfilled.

2). Israel Is Destined To Become A Blessing To All The Nations: This obviously has not taken place: *"Thus saith the LORD of hosts; It shall yet come to pass, that there shall come people, and the inhabitants of many cities: And the inhabitants of one city shall go to another, saying, Let us go speedily to pray before* *the LORD, and to seek the LORD of hosts; I will go also. Yea, many people and strong nations shall come to seek the LORD of hosts in Jerusalem, and to pray before the LORD. Thus saith the LORD of hosts; In those days it shall come to pass, that ten men shall take hold out of all languages of the nations, even shall take hold of the skirt of him that is a Jew, saying, We will go with you: for we have heard that God is with you"* (Zechariah 8:20–23).

The good news that the Lord reigns in Jerusalem will spread rapidly. People from all nations will seek the Lord. An unprecedented global revival among the nations will take place because they will have realized that God is with the Jews. The Jewish people are still despised and considered insignificant. The country is brought before national tribunals and stands accused. There seems to be nothing special about Israel to the world at large, so why should this nation be God's people? Because the Bible says:

• *"And many nations shall be joined to the LORD in that day, and shall be my people: and I will dwell in the midst of thee, and thou shalt know that the LORD of hosts hath sent me unto thee"* (Zechariah 2:11);

• *"And it shall come to pass, that every one that is left of all the nations which came against Jerusalem shall even go up from year to year to worship the King, the LORD of hosts, and to keep the feast of tabernacles"* (Zechariah 14:16);

• *"And many people shall go and say, Come ye, and let us go up to the mountain of the LORD, to the house of the God of Jacob; and he will teach us of his ways, and we will walk in his paths: for out of Zion shall go forth the law, and the word of the LORD from Jerusalem"* (Isaiah 2:3).

What Does The Future Hold?

The effects that result from the future millennium of peace will bring about unimagined blessings. The people, along with the debris of Jerusalem, will be raised up: *"Thus saith the LORD of hosts, There shall yet old men and old women dwell in the streets of Jerusalem, and every man with his staff in his hand for very age. And the streets of the city shall be full of boys and girls playing in the streets thereof"* (Zechariah 8:4–5).

Jeremiah wept and lamented after Jerusalem's destruction: *"The elders of the daughter of Zion sit upon the ground, and keep silence: they have cast up dust upon their heads; they have girded themselves with sackcloth: the virgins of Jerusalem hang down their heads to the ground...The tongue of the sucking child cleaveth to the roof of his mouth for thirst: the young children ask bread, and no man breaketh it unto them"* (Lamentations 2:10; 4:4). Certainly this was not something that was soon forgotten. How this promise must have encouraged them! Its as though

God saw their sorrow and gave them a new hope for the future: God will bring new life into being, people will live to be old, and the children will be able to play in the streets again without fear of terrorists (compare to Isaiah 65:19 onward). This is inconceivable today, but it will happen.

Not only will the city, the people and the nations prosper, but the land will as well: *"But now I will not be unto the residue of this people as in the former days, saith the LORD of hosts. For the seed shall be prosperous; the vine shall give her fruit, and the ground shall give her increase, and the heavens shall give their dew; and I will cause the remnant of this people to possess all these things"* (Zechariah 8:11–12). New life emerges when God grants forgiveness. As a result, nature will be restored: *"...and I will remove the iniquity of that land in one day. In that day, saith the LORD of hosts, shall ye call every man his neighbour under the vine and under the fig tree"* (Zechariah 3:9–10). In a world of terrorist attacks and threats of war and destruction, peace will spring up, which the Lord realized on Calvary's Cross, and will bring to its completion at His return.

This promise has a very earnest aspect that we must not ignore. The Lord said: *"...I will not be unto the residue of this people as in the former days"* (Zechariah 8:11), and the Apostle Paul said this in Romans 9:27: *"...a remnant* (of the children of Israel) *shall be saved."* Sorrow will turn to joy for this remnant: *"Thus saith the LORD of hosts; The fast of the fourth month, and the fast of the fifth, and the fast of the seventh, and the fast of the tenth, shall be to the house of Judah joy and gladness, and cheerful feasts; therefore love the truth and peace"* (Zechariah 8:19). Verse 19 returns to the question found in Zechariah 7:3 and the negative answer found in chapter 7:5–6. But now Israel receives a positive answer which goes beyond what she imagined: Two fasts were added to those in the fifth and seventh months; namely, those in the fourth and tenth months. These fasts will become feasts.

God can turn sorrow into joy! When a person receives the Lord's forgiveness, nothing is the same. The Lord's parable of the prodigal son makes this point clear: *"For this my son was dead, and is alive again: he was lost, and is found. And they began to be merry"* (Luke 15:24). This parable refers to Israel, but it also applies to every person who returns to God in repentance and follows Jesus. The Lord said that no one can take away the joy He gives us (John 16:22).

What Can We Learn From History For The Future?

These tremendous promises and prospects for Israel's future may not be turned into a license to live a superficial life, which is why the words we read in Zechariah 7:9–10 are repeated in chapter 8:16–17,

"These are the things that ye shall do; Speak ye every man the truth to his neighbour; execute the judgment of truth and peace in your gates: And let none of you imagine evil in your hearts against his neighbour; and love no false oath: for all these are things that I hate, saith the Lord." And the end of verse 19 says, *"...therefore love the truth and peace."* Israel's future will be determined by God, but the Israelites are to seek Him.

A sanctified life is required to have fellowship with God. Nobody can sincerely believe in God's goodness and simultaneously desire to live in sin. Faith must be proven by our deeds. We cannot claim to love God and at the same time, hate our brothers. We cannot say that we are following the Lord, yet try to deceive Him. We cannot praise the truth of God's Word, and lie, *"Who is a wise man and endued with knowledge among you? let him shew out of a good conversation his works with meekness of wisdom. But if ye have bitter envying and strife in your hearts, glory not, and lie not against the truth"* (James 3:13–14). The life of a born-again believer must reflect an attitude and behavior compatible with this high calling.

CHAPTER 11

THE WAVES OF THE ENDTIMES

"The burden of the word of the LORD in the land of Hadrach, and Damascus shall be the rest thereof: when the eyes of man, as of all the tribes of Israel, shall be toward the LORD. And Hamath also shall border thereby; Tyrus, and Zidon, though it be very wise. And Tyrus did build herself a strong hold, and heaped up silver as the dust, and fine gold as the mire of the streets. Behold, the LORD will cast her out, and he will smite her power in the sea; and she shall be devoured with fire...When I have bent Judah for me, filled the bow with Ephraim, and raised up thy sons, O Zion, against thy sons, O Greece, and made thee as the sword of a mighty man" (Zechariah 9:1–4 and 13).

Some expositors of God's Word believe that the word "Hadrach" in verse 1, which only occurs this one time in the entire Bible, is related to the Hebrew word *chadar,* which means "surround." They believe that "Hadrach" is a representation of the nations that oppose God's people and surround them in hostility (compare with Ezekiel 28:26). Today it seems as though everything we hear or read involves Israel in some way, and that God is using these incidents as a forewarning to the nations.

On the other hand, the word "Hamath," found in verse 2, is seen as the northwestern portion of Syria, a gateway for Israel's enemies to the north.

The Bible explicitly pronounces the downfall of these nations. Tyre's destruction is particularly emphasized in Zechariah 9 and refers to Alexander the Great in 332 B.C. (verse 13). This destruction becomes a prophetic picture of God's judgments upon the rich nations in the end-times. Therefore, we could rightly translate the word "Tyre" with the words "global world."

Let's consider these verses in the context of Scripture and consider the word "Tyre" in a little more detail in order to better understand the historical situation.

The most compact word of judgment over Tyre is found in Ezekiel chapters 26–28. These three chapters containing God's wrath upon Tyre are simultaneously framed by God's view of Israel.

Ezekiel 26:1–2: *"And it came to pass in the eleventh year, in the first day of the month, that the word of the LORD came unto me, saying, Son of man, because that Tyrus hath said against Jerusalem, Aha, she is broken that was the gates of the people: she is turned unto me: I shall be replenished, now she is laid waste."* Three chapters proclaiming judgment follow, and the message concerning Tyre ends with God's words in Ezekiel 28:25–26: *"Thus saith the LORD God; When I shall have gathered the house of Israel from the people among whom they are scattered, and shall be sanctified in them in the sight of the heathen, then shall they dwell in their land that I have given to my servant Jacob. And they shall dwell safely therein, and shall build houses, and plant vineyards; yea, they shall dwell with confidence, when I have executed judgments upon all those that despise them round about them; and they shall know that I am the LORD their God."* We reverently note that God will judge the nations in accordance with their attitude toward Israel. And we also see that the Lord has not lost sight of His people.

The nations that desire to harm Israel will perish, but the Jews, God's covenantal people, will remain for eternity (Daniel 7:18 and 27).

Zechariah chapter 9 also begins with the words, *"The burden of the word of the LORD,"* and ends with the words, *"And the LORD their God shall save them in that day as the flock of his people: for they shall be as the stones of a crown, lifted up as an ensign upon his land. For how great is his goodness, and how great is his beauty! corn shall make the young men cheerful, and new wine the maids"* (verses 16–17). The Word of God stands as firm as a rock and will remain for eternity! The nations may grit their teeth, but all enmity against God and His people will fail on account of this Word. Someone wrote these words in connection with the terrorist attacks of September 11th, 2001:

"It should shake us up that it becomes clearer and clearer how closely the world-wide terrorist threat is connected with a tiny land which is not even as large as the state of New York and has far less inhabitants. The fact that Israel is continually being made the center of world politics is hardly to be explained rationally. And when it is revealed that the desired peace ultimately fails over the existence of Israel, the great union of states against terror could very quickly turn against Israel" (Zechariah 12:3).

Tyre: An Example From History

A careful reading of Ezekiel 26:1–14 explains that Tyre was a city in Lebanon, situated on the Mediterranean Sea. The city was well known as the center of world trade at that time. Trade routes from southern Arabia to the Orient passed through Tyre. All shipping traffic in the Mediterranean, the gigantic fleet of Phoenician ships, was concentrated in Tyre. There the wares were loaded and brought to Europe, among other places. The Phoenicians possessed the colony of Tarshish in Spain, which we know from the book of Jonah. The entire Mediterranean trade was controlled by the city of Tyre.

King Hiram of Tyre's friendship with Solomon turned into profound hatred for Israel centuries later. When Babylon destroyed Jerusalem under Nebuchadnezzar's rule in 586 B.C., Tyre rejoiced and said mockingly: *"Aha, she is broken that was the gates of the people: she is turned unto me: I shall be replenished, now she is laid waste"* (Ezekiel 26:2). Jerusalem lay on the trade route from south to north; therefore, she also played an important role as the *"...gates of the people."*

Jerusalem's collapse meant more custom duty for Tyre on products coming from Arabia to the north and east: *"She is turned unto me: I shall be replenished, now she is laid waste."* Those who have much always want more. Now an economic rival had fallen. The situation in our day is reflected here. For instance, it is well known that western firms in Austria, France, Germany and Holland sold technology to Syria to develop and produce biological and chemical weapons.

Tyre trusted in her economic power and strength: *"And say unto Tyrus, O thou that art situate at the entry of the sea, which art a merchant of the people for many isles, Thus saith the Lord GOD; O Tyrus, thou hast said, I am of perfect beauty. Thy borders are in the midst of the seas, thy builders have perfected thy beauty"* (Ezekiel 27:3–4).

Today, almost all decisions are made on the basis of economic advantage; therefore, people are pro-Israel if it is to their economic advantage, but they turn against the country as soon as it appears to be economically inopportune. Even the invasion of Gog, in the land of Israel will be motivated by economic interests (Ezekiel 38:10–13).

In the Scofield Bible translation, Ezekiel 27 is compared to Babylon's downfall in Revelation 12, where the collapse of the gigantic world economic system is described (compare to Ezekiel 27:32–35). In Ezekiel 28, Tyre is accused of becoming proud of her knowledge. In this context, Tyre illustrates Satan's fall. Actually, he is identified with Tyre. Satan ruled the world from within the city walls of Tyre.

This example shows that while the nations strive after riches, power and knowledge, they open themselves up to be led more by Satan than by God. The Word of God as a measure for human coexistence is rejected, and has been replaced by money. Who is behind this capitalistic way of thinking? Who is behind the global rearmament? Who is behind the practice of abortion, genetic engineering and cloning? Who is behind the New World Order or globalization?

Paul warned the Colossians, *"Mortify therefore your members which are upon the earth; fornication, uncleanness, inordinate affection, evil concupiscence, and covetousness, which is idolatry: For which things' sake the wrath of God cometh on the children of disobedience"* (Colossians 3:5–6). All sins ultimately culminate in covetousness. This is the idolatry of our day that brings God's judgment upon us. James wrote, *"Your gold and silver is cankered; and the rust of them shall be a witness against you, and shall eat your flesh as it were fire. Ye have heaped treasure together for the last days"* (James 5:3).

As Tyre is put on par with Satan's picture and actions in Ezekiel 28, it becomes clear that the history of this city has not ended. Instead, her development, as long as Satan exists, will continue through all nations to eternity. Security, riches and intellectual achievements count today; these make mankind so proud. In most cases, they lead to forsaking God, His Word and His people. Earthly splendors are usually in Satan's service and are offered by him to deceive mankind (Luke 4:5–8). Satan is the invisible ruler over all worldly glitter, which leads to pride. Revelation 13 explains how the economy (buying and selling) becomes the means of the Antichrist's control. In politics, only that which brings advantage, security and money count, even at the cost of others (for instance, at Israel's cost, or that of the unborn baby, the old or the sick). Capital has more power than politics today. I read the following on this subject:

"World trade has begun to take the power out of the hands of political leaders. Investments, mega fusions, communications...these are the catchwords of our time. Companies work on a global basis. Their head offices are located in the metropolis of the financially strongest states...People concentrate on the mega cities. There is trade, work and money" (*Ethos* 11/01).

The Message Of Judgment To Tyre

The first part of the message of judgment to Tyre describes how the catastrophe comes over the city through the nations in phases (Ezekiel 26:7–11). The second part describes the attack of the Babylonians by Nebuchadnezzar (Ezekiel 26:7–11), and the third describes the attack by Greece (Ezekiel 26:12–14).

The detail in which God's prophecies have been fulfilled over the centuries becomes apparent: *"Remember the former things of old: for I am God...Declaring the end from the beginning, and from ancient times the things that are not yet done, saying, My counsel shall stand, and I will do all my pleasure...I have spoken it, I will also bring it to pass; I have purposed it, I will also do it"* (Isaiah 46:9–13).

Nebuchadnezzar Attacks

The Babylonians went to work ten years after the Assyrians attacked Tyre. Nebuchadnezzar came to Tyre and besieged it in 585 B.C., one year after Jerusalem fell, and shortly after Tyre mocked Jerusalem and rejoiced at her fall. But the city was practically invincible. The siege lasted for thirteen years, until Tyre was finally destroyed in 572 B.C. But when Nebuchadnezzar broke into the city, he found out that the inhabitants fled to the island 800 meters away. They had gotten away with almost all of their riches and had built a new city. Nebuchadnezzar was forced to give up because he had no fleet. Ezekiel 26:7–11 was fulfilled through Nebuchadnezzar's attack, but further prophecies in Ezekiel 26:12 and forward were not fulfilled.

Thirteen years of military service and hardly any pay. This is also described in Ezekiel 29:17–20: *"And it came to pass in the seven and twentieth year, in the first month, in the first day of the month, the word of the LORD came unto me, saying, Son of man, Nebuchadnezzar king of Babylon caused his army to serve a great service against Tyrus: every head was made bald, and every shoulder was peeled: yet had he no wages, nor his army, for Tyrus, for the service that he had served against it: Therefore thus saith the Lord GOD; Behold, I will give the land of Egypt unto Nebuchadnezzar king of Babylon; and he shall take her multitude, and take her spoil, and take her prey; and it shall be the wages for his army. I have given him the land of Egypt for his labor wherewith he served against it, because they wrought for me, saith the Lord GOD."* With great reverence, we see the extent God holds the fate of the nations in His hand!

The Greeks: Executors Of Judgment

"When I have bent Judah for me, filled the bow with Ephraim, and raised up thy sons, O Zion, against thy sons, O Greece, and made thee as the sword of a mighty man" (Zechariah 9:13). Judgment came upon Tyre continuously: *"Therefore thus saith the Lord GOD; Behold, I am against thee, O Tyrus, and will cause many nations to come up against thee, as the sea causeth his waves to come up"* (Ezekiel 26:3), until Tyre was finally destroyed and the Word of God fulfilled.

- The Persians came in 539 B.C. After they conquered the Babylonian Empire, they also conquered Tyre.
- A king of Cyprus fought against the new city of Tyre in 370 B.C.
- Alexander the Great finally came from Greece in 332 B.C. He fulfilled the still outstanding prophecy of God almost 250 years after Nebuchadnezzar.

In order to conquer Tyre, Alexander built a dam from the mainland. It was 800 meters long, 60 meters wide, and up to 200 meters deep. For the dam, he used the remains of Tyre, such as the walls, stones, wood, earth, debris and even the dust: *"And they shall make a spoil of thy riches, and make a prey of thy merchandise: and they shall break down thy walls, and destroy thy pleasant houses: and they shall lay thy stones and thy timber and thy dust in the midst of the water...And I will make thee like the top of a rock: thou shalt be a place to spread nets upon; thou shalt be built no more: for I the LORD have spoken it, saith the Lord GOD"* (Ezekiel 26:12 and 14). Alexander the Great conquered Tyre after seven months; 30,000 people were sold as slaves, 2,000 men were crucified and 8,000 were killed. The Bible is always fulfilled. The pronouns "he" and "his" in Ezekiel 26:7–11 always refer to Nebuchadnezzar. Yet, in Ezekiel 26:12, the pronoun is changed to "they," which refers to the Greeks. We can only stand amazed at the precision of God's Word.

Now God's prophecies were literally fulfilled. Ancient

Tyre had become a bare rock and was never rebuilt. Actually, ancient Tyre is hardly identifiable by archaeologists: *"I will make thee a terror, and thou shalt be no more: though thou be sought for, yet shalt thou never be found again, saith the Lord GOD"* (Ezekiel 26:21). The NIV renders the first part of this verse as: *"I will bring you to a horrible end and you will be no more."* The surrounding nations were so shocked that they voluntarily surrendered to Alexander: *"Now shall the isles tremble in the day of thy fall; yea, the isles that are in the sea shall be troubled at thy departure"* (Ezekiel 26:18).

However, we must note that Ezekiel's prophecy sounds like one continual prophecy, as if judgment upon Tyre would be fulfilled within a few years and all at one time. But there were various fulfillments before the main fulfillment actually took place. Two hundred and fifty years passed between Nebuchadnezzar and Alexander the Great. When Nebuchadnezzar departed, the people of Tyre could have said, "We got away with it. Ezekiel's message was not literally fulfilled. Now we can carry on!" But the Lord's prophecy had to be fulfilled completely, only it took place in phases: *"My counsel shall stand, and I will do all my pleasure"* (Isaiah 46:10).

The Fall of Tyre — An Example For The Western World

The attacks on the World Trade Center towers and their subsequent collapse left the whole world with a feeling of consternation. Most nations felt sympathy because it had happened to the so-called "Christian" world. The economy seems to have recovered from the initial shock, yet the next wave could break over us at any time. Haggai 2:6–7 says: *"For thus saith the LORD of hosts; Yet once, it is a little while, and I will shake the heavens, and the earth, and the sea, and the dry land; And I will shake all nations."*

The wave of AIDS has passed over us, followed by the wave of Chernobyl. Then came the Gulf War and the BSE (Mad Cow Disease), and that was followed by the wave of terror over the United States. We do not know what will follow after a shorter or longer period of time. Ultimately, however, the waves of the turbulent sea of nations will bring about the flood of the Great Tribulation.

In 1998, an American author wrote:

"...It is no longer midnight...it is already past midnight! ...From what I know of the Bible, I have to conclude that God's judgment can break out over us any day now. Perhaps some madman or an ignored anonymous warning will be the factor that sets it in motion. It may be that we experience even greater affluence in the future, but ultimately the fire of God's wrath awaits us!"

In its March 2000 edition, German news magazine, *Der Spiegel,* reported on the power play of world trade, and compared the megalomania of the economy with the megalomania of man at the time of the building of the Tower of Babel. German Bible commentator, Adolf Pohl, wrote this concerning Nebuchadnezzar's Babylon:

"In Babylon the merchants were not only powerful, but they also exercised mental and emotional strength. Their merchant's ideology permeated everything, changed everything into turnover and profit...morals and ethics were at rock bottom."

Revelation 18 makes it clear that the Babylon of the last days is determined by the economy of world trade and that this is under the rule of a totalitarian anti-Christian system. Can the world events taking place in our day be more precisely summarized than with the term 'Babylon'?

What Is The Message For Us?

Tyre is a picture that can very easily apply to the nations of the endtimes. The free world is characterized by power, knowledge and pride. However, Tyre is also a picture of the endtimes, because therein Satan's actions are described (Ezekiel 28). He will develop his power in the nations of the endtimes.

A first warning is that endtime judgments predicted by God will come upon us like waves (Ezekiel 26:3). Jesus described deception, wars, the rising of one nation against another, disease, famines and earthquakes as *"...the beginning of sorrows"* (Matthew 24:4–8). The nations' increasing hatred for Israel, an increase of lawlessness and great distress, and the shaking of heaven and earth are further phases of the endtime judgments before Jesus returns. The waves of judgment will come upon our world with increasing severity. Luke 21:25 applies in this connection: *"...and upon the earth distress of nations, with perplexity; the sea and the waves roaring."*

A second warning lies in the fact that we should come to see that God is Lord through the judgments (Ezekiel 26:6 and 28:23–24). God has brought cities, nations and empires to their downfall throughout history in order to establish His testimony. He has had kings appointed and dethroned — Pharaoh in Egypt, Nebuchadnezzar in Babylon and Cyrus in Persia. Even Gog, from the land of Magog, will be led by God to the mountains of Israel in order to be destroyed. May our world realize that there is a God! *"I am God and there is none else; I am God, and there is none like me, Declaring the end from the beginning, and from ancient times the things that are not yet done,"* He says of Himself in Isaiah 46:9–10. Biblically speaking, judgment means that God allows sin to run its course and that He withdraws His restraining hand.

A third warning is that the God of Israel does not allow His people to perish. After God ended His message of judgment to Syria, Tyre and the Philistines in Zechariah 9, we read of Israel: *"And the LORD shall be seen over them, and his arrow shall go forth as the lightning: and the Lord GOD shall blow the trumpet, and shall go with whirlwinds of the south. The Lord of hosts shall defend them...And the LORD their God shall save them in that day as the flock of his people: for they shall be as the stones of a crown, lifted up as an ensign upon his land.*

For how great is his goodness, and how great is his beauty! corn shall make the young men cheerful, and new wine the maids" (verses 14–15a and 16–17).

Satan will release his rage in a flood of waves against the Jewish people in the endtimes (Revelation 12:15 onward). He wants to exterminate Israel, God's holy testimony on earth. But he will never achieve this!

The fourth warning is that every person should surrender his or her rebellious heart to God's offer of salvation because the Lord says: *"I am God, and there is none like me...I have spoken it, I will also bring it to pass; I have purposed it, I will also do it. Hearken unto me, ye stout-hearted, that are far from righteousness: I bring near my righteousness; it shall not be far off, and my salvation shall not tarry"* (Isaiah 46:9–13). God tells us to whom we should listen, and where our safety lies in these troubled times: *"Hearken unto me..."* He also tells us where we stand by nature: Far from His righteousness, *"ye...that are far from righteousness."*

The Lord doesn't leave us where we are. He tells us that He has done everything so that we do not have to remain as we are: *"I bring near my righteousness; it shall not be far off."* He did this in the redeeming death and resurrection of Jesus Christ. Those who grasp this by faith will experience that His salvation never comes too late: *"...my salvation shall not tarry."*

The people of Tyre had stubborn hearts where God was concerned. They felt safe, they had everything they needed and they were proud and arrogant. Satan dwelt within the walls of Tyre and had his way with the city's inhabitants. The people of the city were deceived into a false sense of security. They thought they didn't need God and only thought of an increase in material things. Satan won their hearts and made them rebellious. Is that the case with you? Are you ruled by greed, selfishness and pride? Do you only live for yourself? Remember, those who do not surrender to Jesus Christ will perish.

My dear reader, you have two possibilities where your life is concerned: You can be like Daniel, who used his wisdom, intelligence and position for God and His cause, or you can be like the King of Tyre, who only used his wisdom for the things of this world and excluded God from His life: *"Behold, thou art wiser than Daniel; there is no secret that they can hide from thee: With thy wisdom and with thine understanding thou hast gotten thee riches, and hast gotten gold and silver into thy treasures"* (Ezekiel 28:3–4). You can put yourself at the disposal of the true God of heaven and earth, or serve the god of this world. Have you made your choice? If not, do so now!

C H A P T E R   1 2

HOW GOD WILL SOLVE THE
ISRAELI-PALESTINIAN CONFLICT

"Ashkelon shall see it, and fear; Gaza also shall see it, and be very sorrowful, and Ekron; for her expectation shall be ashamed; and the king shall perish from Gaza, and Ashkelon shall not be inhabited. And a bastard shall dwell in Ashdod, and I will cut off the pride of the Philistines. And I will take away his blood out of his mouth, and his abominations from between his teeth: but he that remaineth, even he, shall be for our God, and he shall be as a governor in Judah, and Ekron as a Jebusite. And I will encamp about mine house because of the army, because of him that passeth by, and because of him that returneth: and no oppressor shall pass through them any more: for now have I seen with mine eyes. Rejoice greatly, O daughter of Zion; shout, O daughter of Jerusalem: behold, thy King cometh unto thee: he is just, and having salvation; lowly, and riding upon an ass, and upon a colt

the foal of an ass" (Zechariah 9:5–9).

We can only explain present-day history when we consider the spiritual background. The condition for this is that we believe the Bible and consult it for an explanation of history. In order to be able to explain the conflict between the Israelis and Palestinians, we must go right back to the origin of the Jews and Arabs.

The Philistines In Prophecy

The Philistines no longer exist in their original form, just as the Canaanites, Edomites, Moabites, Ammonites, Assyrians, Amelekites, Gog, Meshech, etc., no longer exist. But their territories have been partly preserved, and spiritually, their lines continue to the endtimes. There are many prophetic statements about nations that have disappeared which have to be fulfilled in the endtimes. People have mingled and through this, in contrast to Israel, the races are not pure-blooded any more. For instance, Moab, Edom and Ammon make up present-day Jordan. Assyria is Syria, and the people of the land of Gog from Magog also have different names today. Persia is Iran, and Babylon is Iraq. The Bible does not identify them with their current names, but with the names they were known as then. These are mostly nations whose people became Islamic and whose enmity and hatred towards Israel and Judaism have remained to the present day. Therefore they occur mostly in endtime prophecies and play an important role. So this is more about geographic connections than it is about the people who live in these places.

For example, let's consider Balak, the Moabite King. Balaam said to him, *"And now, behold, I go unto my people: come therefore, and I will advertise thee what this people shall do to thy people in the latter days"* (Numbers 24:14). It is not a coincidence that many ancient biblical sites are in the spotlight today. These locations are hotly-contested by the Palestinians and cast great light on the prophetic Word. Think of Jericho as a picture of the conquest of the Promised Land on the grounds of God's promises. Or Hebron, the place where Abraham pitched his tent after God had promised him the land (Genesis 13:14–18). Or Bethlehem, the home-town of David and birthplace of Jesus. Sichem, which is present-day Nablus, and the largest Palestinian town in West Jordan, is where God promised Abraham the entire land of Canaan (Genesis 12:6–7). So we can say that the Palestinians are the spiritual continuation of the Philistines of biblical times.

Many prophecies predict judgment upon the Philistines. Many threats of judgment have been fulfilled in the course of history. For instance, David overcame the Philistines when he slew Goliath; they also remained subdued under King Solomon's reign. Later on, King Hezekiah, conquered them again. But after the division of the kingdom under King Rehoboam, they were back again. During Jehoram's time, they plundered Judah and Jerusalem (2nd Chronicles 21:16–17).

The Egyptians also conquered the Philistines at certain times (Jeremiah 47). Later, they came under Assyrian rule, then under Babylonian and Persian rules. Moreover, the Philistines were conquered by the Greeks under Alexander the Great. In prophecy they appear on the scene again right up to the endtimes. Therefore, the actual endtime judgment upon the Philistines is still unfulfilled. This is clear from the following texts:

- *"Because the Philistines have dealt by revenge, and have taken vengeance with a despiteful heart, to destroy it for the old hatred; Therefore thus saith the Lord GOD; Behold, I will stretch out mine hand upon the Philistines, and I will cut off the Cherethims, and destroy the remnant of the sea coast. And I will execute great vengeance upon them with furious rebukes; and they shall know that I am the LORD, when I shall lay my vengeance upon them"* (Ezekiel 25:15–17). So here we have an old hatred of the Philistines for Israel, which will only cease when Jesus returns. This line of hatred continues today through the Palestinians. It is not by coincidence that the word "Philistine" is identical with the word "Palestinian." The devil is behind this hatred. Hatred will cease on-

174

ly when he is bound (Revelation 20:1–3). The terrorism carried out by Palestinian organizations will be judged and destroyed by God.

• Zephaniah goes beyond the imminent events of that time, such as the destruction of Jerusalem, to proclaim the *"day of the Lord,"* the time of the Great Tribulation (Zephaniah 1:3). He prophesied, *"The great day of the LORD is near, it is near, and hasteth greatly, even the voice of the day of the LORD: the mighty man shall cry there bitterly. That day is a day of wrath, a day of trouble and distress, a day of wasteness and desolation, a day of darkness and gloominess, a day of clouds and thick darkness"* (Zephaniah 1:14–15). And he instructed: *"Seek ye the LORD, all ye meek of the earth, which have wrought his judgment; seek righteousness, seek meekness: it may be ye shall be hid in the day of the LORD's anger"* (Zephaniah 2:3). Concerning the Philistines, it then says, *"For Gaza shall be forsaken, and Ashkelon a desolation: they shall drive out Ashdod at the noon day, and Ekron shall be rooted up. Woe unto the inhabitants of the sea coast, the nation of the Cherethites! the word of the LORD is against you; O Canaan, the land of the Philistines, I will even destroy thee, that there shall be no inhabitant. And the sea coast shall be dwellings and cottages for shepherds, and folds for flocks. And the coast shall be for the remnant of the house of Judah; they shall feed thereupon: in the houses of*

Ashkelon shall they lie down in the evening: for the LORD their God shall visit them and turn away their captivity" (Zephaniah 2:4–7). This will be completely fulfilled *"in the latter days."* For it says in the summary of Zephaniah's statements: *"At that time will I bring you again, even in the time that I gather you: for I will make you a name and a praise among all people of the earth, when I turn back your captivity before your eyes, saith the LORD"* (Zephaniah 3:20).

• We find a similar prophecy in Zechariah 9:5–9, which is included in the beginning of this chapter. These words were partially fulfilled through the victory of the Greeks over Tyre (Zechariah 9:13). All of the surrounding lands were in a state of shock when Alexander the Great destroyed Tyre, a city upon which the Philistines depended (Ezekiel 26:15–18). But Zechariah's prophecy extends far beyond this, up to its main, endtime fulfillment.

The following facts make it clear that this refers to the endtimes:

• These events are connected with the Messiah's return for Israel, the ultimate restoration of His people, and the establishment of His millennium of peace (verses 14 and 16). Moreover, they are about the future blessings in the Messianic kingdom of peace (verse 10).

They reveal that the nations will at last bury their weapons of war and never again will an oppressor pass through their land (verse 8). Many oppressors passed through Israel after these words were written following the Babylonian captivity. For instance, the Greeks under Alexander the Great, Antiochus Epiphanes, the Romans, the Muslims, the Crusaders and the Turks. If, according to the prophetic Word, no oppressor will ever pass through Israel again, then this refers to the time of the Messianic kingdom.

• They are related to God's abiding protection of Israel in the millennium of peace (verse 8).

The Origin Of The Philistines

The Philistines were an Indo-European, seafaring people who originally came to the Middle East from the Aegean via Crete and Cyprus. They came from Crete (Caphtor) to Egypt and wandered from there through the wilderness to Canaan in the Gaza Strip. They possessed the five main cities there: Gaza, Ashkelon, Ashdod, Ekron and Gath (Joshua 13:2–3).

The origin of the Philistines is mentioned in Jeremiah 47:4: *"Because of the day that cometh to spoil all the Philistines, and to cut off from Tyrus and Zidon every helper that remaineth: for the LORD will spoil the Philistines, the remnant of the country of Caphtor."* Amos 9:7 says: *"Are ye not as children of the Ethiopians unto me, O children of Israel? saith the LORD. Have not I brought up Israel out of the land of Egypt? and the Philistines from Caphtor, and the*

Syrians from Kir?" A description of their stay and exodus from Egypt is found in Genesis 10:13–14: *"And Mizraim begat Ludim, and Anamim, and Lehabim, and Naphtuhim, And Pathrusim, and Casluhim, (out of whom came Philistim,) and Caphtorim."* Mizraim was Egypt's patriarch. Egypt is still called Mizraim today in Hebrew.

The various tribes of Egypt are mentioned in the above-quoted verses 13–14. The Philistines had settled among the Egyptian tribe of Casluhim and left from there, *"...and Casluhim, (out of whom came Philistim)."* We read of their entrance into the Gaza Strip in Deuteronomy 2:23: *"And the Avims which dwelt in Hazerim, even unto Azzah, the Caphtorims, which came forth out of Caphtor, destroyed them, and dwelt in their stead."*

Parallels With Israel

We know that the Philistines were always Israel's most persistent enemies, particularly because they lived in the midst of Israel. This is no different today. Moreover, their history seems to have a devilish parallel to Israel. The devil always attempts to imitate the true God by creating a similar, yet false, alternative to the truth.

Consider these antonyms:
- Christ – Antichrist
- Biblical prophets – false prophets

- Genuine born-again Christianity – false, nominal Christianity
- The Bible – an anti-Bible (Koran, Book of Mormon)

The devil confronts the prophecies of the Holy Scriptures with fortune-telling and clairvoyance, and salvation with spiritual alternatives through old and new religions (Buddhism, Hinduism, New Age, Esoteric, etc.)

Thus, the Philistines have certain similarities with the Israelites:

- They came to Egypt just like the Israelites.
- They left Egypt just like the Israelites.
- They came to the land of Canaan just like the Israelites.

This seems like the devil's blow against God who promised this land to Abraham (Genesis 12:5–7, 13:15–17, 15:13–14 and 18, and 17:8).

The battle of the Philistines over Israel's promised inheritance continues throughout history to this present day, and is reaching its climax. Marwan Barghouti, leader of the Fatah terrorists, said that Intifada's first goal of the rebellion is the founding of a Palestinian state with Jerusalem as its capital. He added that they had big plans to banish the Jews and conquer Israel.

The Great Difference

There is a great difference between Israel's exodus from Egypt and entrance into the Promised Land, and the Philistines' exodus from Egypt and entrance into

Canaan, which must not be overlooked. *"And it came to pass, when Pharaoh had let the people go, that God led them not through the way of the land of the Philistines, although that was near; for God said, Lest peradventure the people repent when they see war, and they return to Egypt: But God led the people about, through the way of the wilderness of the Red sea: and the children of Israel went up harnessed out of the land of Egypt"* (Exodus 13:17–18). God didn't lead the Israelites into the Promised Land by the easiest route. Instead, He led His people from the Nile delta down through the Red Sea, through the Sinai desert and finally through the Jordan and into the Promised Land.

The Jordan is the "river of death" that flows into the Dead Sea. It is a picture of the Cross of Christ, His death, His resurrection and the new birth a person experiences through a conversion to Him. Here we find forgiveness, redemption and liberation to enter into the Promised Land: Crucified with Christ and risen to eternal life with God the Father! We can only reach this heavenly goal through Jesus.

God wanted the Israelites to burn all the bridges to their old lives in Egypt; therefore, He led them through the Red Sea and the Jordan. This is a symbol of baptism into Christ's death for us. The Egyptian army that pursued Israel drowned in the sea. This symbolizes that the Lord conquered Satan and the powers of darkness.

To "pass through" the Jordan means to go through the strait gate on the narrow way, not the wide, comfortable way around the Jordan. The Philistines didn't take this path through the Jordan; they wandered alongside the Mediterranean to the Gaza Strip. Therefore, they have no claim to the Promised Land, even today. If we apply this to Christianity, this means that born-again Christians, who make up the true Church, have passed through the Jordan. They have been converted to Jesus Christ and have been baptized. They have died with Him and have been raised. On the other hand, nominal Christians merely appropriate a "Christian heritage" for themselves going through the Jordan of the Cross of Christ. They don't believe there is a need for conversion. As far as they are concerned, it is sufficient to wear a Christian "cloak." However, this cloak doesn't give them the right to the Promised Land, and so they will ultimately be cast out. We find this described in Matthew 22:11–13, *"And when the king came in to see the guests, he saw there a man which had not on a wedding garment: And he saith unto him, Friend, how camest thou in hither not having a wedding garment? And he was speechless. Then said the king to the servants, Bind him hand and foot, and take him away, and cast him into outer darkness; there shall be weeping and gnashing of teeth."*

Just as the Philistines (the Palestinians) contest Israel's right to the land and cause much trouble for them, nominal Christianity creates grave problems for true Christianity. Nominal "Christians" are not on Israel's side.

The Judgment Upon The Philistines

We have read that the Philistines will be judged in the last days. This judgment seems to be approaching in the form of a war. How long will God look at the activities carried out by the Palestinian terror groups? In the following texts, we are told what will happen in the future, but they do not tell us exactly when:

1. The king shall perish from Gaza (Zechariah 9:5).

2. The land of the Philistines will be given to the Jews, not vice versa: *"Woe unto the inhabitants of the sea coast, the nation of the Cherethites! ...the land of the Philistines, I will even destroy thee, that there shall be no inhabitant. And the sea coast shall be dwellings and cottages for shepherds, and folds for flocks. And the coast shall be for the remnant of the house of Judah; they shall feed thereupon: in the houses of Ashkelon shall they lie down in the evening: for the LORD their God shall visit them, and turn away their captivity"* (Zephaniah 2:5–7).

Will a devastating war take place between the Jews and the Palestinians, from which Israel will emerge as victor? Will a peace agreement be achieved? It is interesting to note that many Arabs, (Palestinians) live in

Judaea. Will these Judean territories belong to the Jews again? It all seems to point to this.

What could this war be like? Zechariah 12:2 may be a reference: *"Behold, I will make Jerusalem a cup of trembling unto all the people round about, when they shall be in the siege both against Judah and against Jerusalem."* If Jerusalem was attacked by the Arab nations around her, then war against Israel could also come from Judaea by the hands of the Arabs living there. Then a simultaneous war against an enemy from without and from within would take place. Zechariah 14:14 says: *"And Judah also shall fight at Jerusalem..."* An exposition of Zechariah 12 will contain greater details about this.

The Philistines' eternal enmity will be punished: *"Thus saith the Lord GOD; Because the Philistines have dealt by revenge, and have taken vengeance with a despiteful heart, to destroy it for the old hatred; Therefore thus saith the Lord GOD; Behold, I will stretch out mine hand upon the Philistines, and I will cut off the Cherethims, and destroy the remnant of the sea coast"* (Ezekiel 25:15–16). Vengeance, spite and hatred for Israel are what drive the Islamic fundamentalists and Palestinian terror organizations, *"... with a despiteful heart, to destroy it for the old hatred."* Isn't this typical since the founding of the PLO by Yasser Arafat in 1964? Terrorism against Israel and international terrorism have been increasing since the

Six-Day War in 1967. How many PLO sponsored terrorist attacks have there been against Israel since then? How many civilians have been brutally murdered? How many suicide attacks have been carried out in complete disregard for human life? In their blind hatred, they even take into account the fact that their own children perish! The PLO is responsible for 40 aircraft hijackings, not to mention other atrocities.

Luke 21:11 says: *"And great earthquakes shall be in divers places, and famines, and pestilences; and fearful sights and great signs shall there be from heaven."* The Amplified Bible translates the phrase *"fearful sights"* as *"sights of terror."*

Haven't these words, penned 2,000 years ago, become extremely relevant in light of the September 11th 2001 attacks? Zechariah 9:7 could also refer to this: *"And I will take away his blood out of his mouth, and his abominations from between his teeth."* This does not refer to idolatry, as other translations show. But isn't the Islamic doctrine, according to which you can get to heaven as a martyr if you blow yourself up in pieces, considered idolatry? Isn't the sacrifice of our own bodies and lives to the demonic exposition of the Koran? Hamas terrorist, Jamal Salim, who was killed by the Jews, persuaded hundreds of young Palestinians to blow themselves up in the name of Allah to liberate Palestine during the last months of his life. "We must sow death in every corner of Israel," he said.

The Remnant Of The Philistines Will Be Saved

God will solve the Israeli-Palestinian conflict through the return of Jesus Christ. Following the judgment, this will result in unimaginable blessing impossible for human beings to bring about themselves.

Zechariah 9:7 says this about the Philistines, *"...But he that remaineth* (of the Philistines), *even he, shall be for our God, and he shall be as a governor in Judah, and Ekron as a Jebusite."*

A couple of the Jebusites were already integrated in Israel in those days. Araunah the Jebusite was a man who bowed down before King David and wanted to give him his possessions so that David could use them as a sacrifice to God. Arauna called David, *"My lord the king,"* in 2nd Samuel 24:18–25. We read that even the Philistines (Pelethites) belonged to David's bodyguards (2nd Samuel 15:18 and 20:7). And when Solomon was made king, the Philistines accompanied him together with Zadok the priest, and prophets Nathan and Benaiah to anoint him (1st Kings 1:38–40). These are all wonderful examples of the future under the rule of Israel's great King, Jesus Christ, the Son of David.

Thus, the Jebusites and Philistines will see that the God of Israel is the one true God, *"...and Ekron as a Jebusite."* Ekron was a Philistine city and means "rooting up." They will be uprooted from out of the ground of hatred and will be planted in the kingdom of God, the kingdom of His dear Son. A note in the German translation of the Bible by a man named Fritz Laubach says:

"Ekron as a Jebusite in that which is said here of the inhabitants of a Philistine city is a wonderful possibility for all who have fought against God's people. Those who were far from God will be converted to Him through judgment and grace, and will receive citizenship among God's people. A hint at what God plans for the completion of the world is that the nations will live in the light of this city and the kings of the earth will bring their glory into her" (Revelation 21:24).

Zechariah 2:11 makes it clear that many other nations will be added: *"And many nations shall be joined to the LORD in that day, and shall be my people: and I will dwell in the midst of thee, and thou shalt know that the LORD of hosts hath sent me unto thee."* Ezekiel 25:17 says this concerning the Philistines: *"And I will execute great vengeance upon them with furious rebukes; and they shall know that I am the Lord, when I shall lay my vengeance upon them."* And Psalm 87:4 says, *"I will make mention of Rahab and Babylon to them that know me: behold Philistia, and Tyre, with Ethiopia; this man was born there."*

In the latter days, a remnant of the Philistines will know the Lord, as we see from the above texts, *"They shall know that I am the Lord...to them that know me.*" The Philistines will come to believe on Him and will be led into the Messianic kingdom via the Cross: *"And this is life eternal, that they might know thee the only true God, and Jesus Christ, whom thou hast sent"* (John 17:3).

This is an earnest warning to every individual, even if you call yourself a Christian. The Lord will lead no one who avoids the Cross into His Kingdom. Only through the death and resurrection of Jesus Christ will we enter into the kingdom of heaven. This means that you must turn to Him; you must make a clear decision to follow Him.

CHAPTER 13

JESUS' FIRST AND SECOND COMING IN ONE VISION

"Rejoice greatly, O daughter of Zion; shout O daughter of Jerusalem: behold, thy King cometh unto thee: he is just, and having salvation; lowly, and riding upon an ass, and upon a colt the foal of an ass. And I will cut off the chariot from Ephraim, and the horse from Jerusalem, and the battle bow shall be cut off: and he shall speak peace unto the heathen: and his dominion shall be from sea even to sea, and from the river even to the ends of the earth. As for thee also, by the blood of thy covenant I have sent forth thy prisoners out of the pit wherein is no water. Turn you to the strong hold, ye prisoners of hope: even to day do I declare that I will render double unto thee; When I have bent Judah for me, filled the bow with Ephraim, and raised up thy sons, O Zion, against thy sons, O Greece, and made thee as the sword of a mighty man. And the LORD shall be seen over them, and his arrow shall go

forth as the lightning: and the Lord GOD shall blow the trumpet, and shall go with whirlwinds of the south. The LORD of hosts shall defend them; and they shall devour, and subdue with sling stones; and they shall drink, and make a noise as through wine; and they shall be filled like bowls, and as the corners of the altar. And the LORD their God shall save them in that day as the flock of his people: for they shall be as the stones of a crown, lifted up as an ensign upon his land. For how great is his goodness, and how great is his beauty! corn shall make the young men cheerful, and new wine the maids" (Zechariah 9:9–17).

The prophets often foretold Jesus' First and Second Comings in one vision. They did not see the valley separating these two events.

Jesus' First Advent

"Rejoice greatly, O daughter of Zion; shout, O daughter of Jerusalem: behold, thy King cometh unto thee: he is just, and having salvation; lowly, and riding upon an ass, and upon a colt the foal of an ass" (Zechariah 9:9). Zechariah's prophecy was literally fulfilled when the Lord came the first time. Jesus commanded His disciples at that time, *"And when they drew nigh unto Jerusalem, and were come to Bethphage, unto the mount of Olives, then sent Jesus two disciples, Saying unto them, Go into the village over against you, and straightway ye shall find an ass tied,*

and a colt with her: loose them, and bring them unto me. And if any man say ought unto you, ye shall say, The Lord hath need of them, and straightway he will send them. All this was done, that it might be fulfilled which was spoken by the prophet, saying, Tell ye the daughter of Sion, Behold, thy King cometh unto thee, meek, and sitting upon an ass, and a colt the foal of an ass. And the disciples went, and did as Jesus commanded them, And brought the ass, and the colt, and put on them their clothes, and they set him thereon" (Matthew 21:1–7). It is certainly not without prophetic significance that God ordered that a donkey, in contrast to all other animals but in the same way as man, could be redeemed through a substitutionary lamb. All the firstborn among the unclean animals had to be redeemed with money or sold; all the firstborn among the clean animals, such as cattle, sheep or goats, had to be sacrificed (compare to Numbers 18:15–17 onwards and Leviticus 27:26–27). Only human beings and donkeys could be redeemed through the sacrifice of a lamb: *"That thou shalt set apart unto the LORD all that openeth the matrix, and every firstling that cometh of a beast which thou hast; the males shall be the LORDs. And every firstling of an ass thou shalt redeem with a lamb; and if thou wilt not redeem it, then thou shalt break his neck; and all the firstborn of man among thy children shalt thou redeem"* (Exodus 13:12–13).

One of the original breeds of donkeys that lived in

the Orient at that time, which also exists even today, features a dark horizontal stripe over its shoulders and a vertical stripe that begins at its neck and travels down its back. From above, it looks as if the ass is carrying a cross on its back. Did the Creator do this purposely?

"And brought the ass, and the colt, and put on them their clothes, and they set him thereon" (Matthew 21:7). This is how Passion Week began. He Who would be crucified in a few days, Whose Cross would read, *"Jesus of Nazareth, the King of the Jews,"* Who would be substitutionally slaughtered for Israel, now sat on the back of an ass. We can already see the Cross in this. Jesus sacrificed Himself for man. Israel's future redemption and liberation are foreshadowed in this picture. There's an indication of what Jesus accomplished on Calvary's Cross for Israel. *"Behold the Lamb of God,"* cried John the Baptist at the sight of Jesus. And it is as though Jesus was saying, *"Bring the donkey to Me; I give My blood for Israel, and for this reason she shall be loosed."*

How literally Zechariah's prophecy was fulfilled! At His First Advent, the Lord appeared as the meek and lowly one (Matthew 11:29) who was obedient to His Father unto death, even the death of the Cross (Philippians 2:5–8). He was the ultimate, eternally valid sin offering for Israel and the entire world. He is also your sin offering. There is no sin for which Jesus did not die. *"Behold the Lamb of God, which taketh away the sin of the world"* (John 1:29).

The Lord was so meek and lowly, so sinless — the true Messiah — that He could sit upon a donkey colt so young that it still was with its mother (Matthew 21:2). Luke said, *"...a colt...whereon yet never man sat"* (Luke 19:30). Normally it is impossible to ride on an untamed colt, but the Lord not only did this (probably even without reins), but also rode through a multitude of people who were calling out to Him and waving palm branches! Yet the ass did not shy or kick out; it behaved as if it were tame beneath the Lord's body. Only the true, supernatural and meek Messiah could ride this colt under these circumstances. This is a beautiful picture of His rule. Where He rules, it is quiet in the midst of noise.

Israel's Present Situation

"And they went their way, and found the colt tied by the door without in a place where two ways met; and they loose him." I believe that three points in this passage could apply to Israel's present situation.

1. The ass was bound. It was controlled by another. Today, the Jews are bound more to the power of America and the European Union than they are to God. The Jewish state is continually forced by Arab nations, and those who support them, to comply with demands that are biblically untenable. Israel is not free because the Messiah's reign has not yet begun. She has to do what the nations lay upon her and cannot move about freely because the time of the nations has not yet ended (Luke 21:24). However, Satan is the prince of the nations (Ephesians 2:2); he is the prince of this world (John 12:31); he is the world ruler (Ephesians 6:12); and he incites the nations against the Jews. Only in this way can the politics of the nations and the media's one-sided reports against Israel be explained.

The individual who has not surrendered his life to Christ is also Satan's possession. Jesus Christ is the only One Who can liberate us from sin, the devil and from all bondage. His blood is the ransom He paid for us. This is why it is vital that the Lord can lay His work upon you and take possession of your life. "Set him free and lead him to me!" Only in Him can we find peace for our hearts. Only under His rule, and the power of His Word, are we safe and without cause for fear.

2. The donkey was outside. The donkey that was bound outside is a picture of man's alienation from God (Ephesians 2:11–13). Israel is in the same position as the nations insofar as she is blind and still living in alienation from God (2nd Corinthians 3:14–16 and Romans 11:25–28). However, the day will come when Israel will be planted in the Messianic kingdom and will come under the Messiah's rule. How many people are still outside, alienated from God and seeking security, yet stand out in the rain? But Jesus has come to take them home!

3. The donkey stood at the crossroad. The Jews will be led to a crossroad where they will have to choose between the Antichrist and Jesus Christ as their Messiah. They will have to choose between the rule of the nations and the rule of God. Today, we are under the impression that Israel is being brought closer to this decisive moment.

The Second Coming Of Christ

In Zechariah 9:10, the eyes of the prophet are lifted from the Lord's First Advent to His Second Coming. Israel is standing at the crossroad between the rule of the nations, the future Antichrist, and the true Messiah. Israel is still bound, she is still outside, and she is still alienated from God. But first, Israel is being led toward the greatest tribulation in her history; she will find herself in a situation from which there is no escape. But then she will receive her sight and set her eyes upon the Lord. Zechariah 9:10 explains how this will happen: *"And I will cut off the chariot from Ephraim, and the horse from Jerusalem, and the battle bow shall be cut off: and he shall speak peace unto the heathen: and his dominion shall be from sea even to sea, and from the river even to the ends of the earth."*

How people are reaching out for peace covenants today! Everyone is crying out for peace, yet there is no peace. There have never been as many terrible wars as there have been in the twentieth century; quite frankly, it doesn't look any better for the twenty-first. Yet, as terrible as they were, the two world wars in the twentieth century were the starting point for Israel's restoration. World War I brought the Jewish people their land and World War II brought them their state. Will a future third world war bring them the Messianic kingdom?

The time of Jesus' return will be a completely new era in which weapons will be turned into plowshares (compare to Isaiah 2:4 and Micah 4:3). This time of the kingdom of peace will embrace the entire world and will include all the nations. No one but Christ can establish a rule of peace that extends over the entire world. The *shalom* (peace) will go forth from Jerusalem, the *"city of peace."* As long as Jerusalem has no peace, the nations will strive in vain and will not rest.

"As for thee also, by the blood of thy covenant I have sent forth thy prisoners out of the pit wherein is no water" (Zechariah 9:11). During Israel's captivity, when they were in dispersion, the Jews were like people imprisoned in a pit without water. This comparison reminds us of Joseph, who was cast into a pit by his brothers, from which he could not free himself (Genesis 37:24). Yet God holds fast to His blood covenant with Israel. He made this covenant with Abraham, and it was sealed by the acceptance of a blood sacrifice (Genesis 15:8–20). A ram was sacri-

ficed in Isaac's place (Genesis 22:13–18). *"The blood of thy covenant"* also reminds us of the countless sacrifices that took place on the grounds of the Sinai covenant that Moses communicated to the people. These are all mere symbols of the blood of the Lamb of God, Jesus Christ, who gave His blood as a sacrifice for Israel. Ultimately, therein lies the reason for Israel's liberation. She will be led to streams of living water again. God's covenant is stronger than any league of nations.

"Turn you to the strong hold, ye prisoners of hope: even to day do I declare that I will render double unto thee" (Zechariah 9:12). The phrase *"prisoners of hope"* reminds us that the Lord will not discard His promises to Israel. Through all tribulation, persecution and dispersion, the Lord will lead His people to freedom and return unto them double. Isaiah prophesied in this direction when he foretold Israel's future: *"For your shame ye shall have double; and for confusion they shall rejoice in their portion: therefore in their land they shall possess the double: everlasting joy shall be unto them"* (Isaiah 61:7).

"When I have bent Judah for me, filled the bow with Ephraim, and raised up thy sons, O Zion, against thy sons, O Greece, and made thee as the sword of a mighty man..." (Zechariah 9:13). This verse probably refers to the Maccabees' victorious battle against Antiochus Epiphanes, the Greek king of Syria, when the

Empire was divided after Alexander the Great. However, it seems that this Jewish victory was used as an example to describe Israel's last victory over her enemies shortly before Jesus returns. Just as the Lord performed a miracle at that time, through His power He will perform a miracle at the end of the days and fight for Israel, which is described in detail in the last three chapters of Zechariah.

"And the LORD shall be seen over them, and his arrow shall go forth as the lightning: and the Lord GOD shall blow the trumpet, and shall go with whirlwinds of the south. The LORD of hosts shall defend them; and they shall devour, and subdue with sling stones; and they shall drink, and make a noise as through wine; and they shall be filled like bowls, and as the corners of the altar. And the LORD their God shall save them in that day as the flock of his people: for they shall be as the stones of a crown, lifted up as an ensign upon his land. For how great is his goodness, and how great is his beauty! corn shall make the young men cheerful, and new wine the maids" (Zechariah 9:14–17). The Lord will intervene triumphantly through His appearance on Israel's behalf and will save His people during the last gathering of the Jews' enemies (Zechariah 12:3–10; 14:1–4, 12). The last two verses are a beautiful picture of the fulfillment of God's promises for His people and His land: *"They will sparkle in his land like jewels in a*

crown. How attractive and beautiful they will be!" (verses 16–17, NIV). How differently God sees the future of His people from how the nations see it! There could not be a more beautiful symbol of God's love for His people and their future than this reference to them as, *"stones of a crown."* When He appears in glory, Israel will be a radiant fruit of the suffering of the Son of God: *"...corn shall make the young men cheerful, and new wine the maids"* (verse 17). Israel will bear fruit in this new era to the glory of her Messiah. Sorrow and suffering, persecution, war and dispersion will be over, and the wine of joy will flow.

Let's return to the beginning of this chapter. He who entered into Jerusalem upon an ass will return victoriously! Jacob saw this new time prophetically and prophesied of it: *"The sceptre shall not depart from Judah, nor a lawgiver from between his feet, until Shiloh come; and unto him shall the gathering of the people be. Binding his foal unto the vine, and his ass's colt unto the choice vine; he washed his garments in wine, and his clothes in the blood of grapes"* (Genesis 49:10–11). This paints a glorious picture of Israel's future. The Lord will return to establish His kingdom in and with Israel: *"Binding his foal unto the vine, and his ass's colt unto the choice vine."* This paints a wonderful picture of the abundant blessings in the millennium of peace. Matthew 21:7, *"And brought the ass, and the colt, and put on them their clothes, and they set him thereon,"* also suggests a picture of this. The ass represents the old Israel, and the colt upon which the Lord sat represents the new, young, restored Israel, upon which He will lay His rule.

At the Lord's coming in glory, the Jews will exclaim the words of the Messianic Psalm 118:26 with all of their hearts. This will be the new, young Israel, like a colt: *"And they that went before, and they that followed, cried, saying, Hosanna; Blessed is he that cometh in the name of the Lord: Blessed be the kingdom of our father David, that cometh in the name of the Lord: Hosanna in the highest. And Jesus entered into Jerusalem, and into the temple..."* (Mark 11:9–11). At that time they asked, *"Who is this?"* (Matthew 21:10), but now they will recognize Him as their Messiah. He will enter the Temple and begin His reign as King, fulfilling Zechariah 9:9: *"Rejoice greatly, O daughter of Zion; shout, O daughter of Jerusalem: behold, thy King cometh unto thee: he is just, and having salvation; lowly, and riding upon an ass, and upon a colt the foal of an ass."*

CHAPTER 14

ISRAEL'S RETURNING SHEPHERD

"Ask ye of the LORD rain in the time of the latter rain; so the LORD shall make bright clouds, and give them showers of rain, to every one grass in the field. For the idols have spoken vanity, and the diviners have seen a lie, and have told false dreams; they comfort in vain: therefore they went their way as a flock, they were troubled, because there was no shepherd. Mine anger was kindled against the shepherds, and I punished the goats: for the LORD of hosts hath visited his flock the house of Judah, and hath made them as his goodly horse in the battle. Out of him came forth the corner, out of him the nail, out of him the battle bow, out of him every oppressor together. And they shall be as mighty men, which tread down their enemies in the mire of the streets in the battle: and they shall fight, because the LORD is with them, and the riders on horses shall be confounded. And I will strengthen the house of Judah, and I will save the house of Joseph,

and I will bring them again to place them; for I have mercy upon them: and they shall be as though I had not cast them off: for I am the LORD their God, and will hear them. And they of Ephraim shall be like a mighty man, and their heart shall rejoice as through wine: yea, their children shall see it, and be glad; their heart shall rejoice in the LORD. I will hiss for them, and gather them; for I have redeemed them: and they shall increase as they have increased. And I will sow them among the people: and they shall remember me in far countries; and they shall live with their children, and turn again. I will bring them again also out of the land of Egypt, and gather them out of Assyria; and I will bring them into the land of Gilead and Lebanon; and place shall not be found for them. And he shall pass through the sea with affliction, and shall smite the waves in the sea, and all the deeps of the river shall dry up: and the pride of Assyria shall be brought down, and the sceptre of Egypt shall depart away. And I will strengthen them in the LORD; and they shall walk up and down in his name, saith the LORD" (Zechariah 10:1–12).

A man named Richard Klick told the following story:

"As a young boy I was invited to a very promising birthday party at the house of a schoolfriend. However, a severe snowstorm had made our village street impassable, and I was not allowed to leave the house. 'Other parents really love their children and let them go!' I cried. My father was hurt by my words. He turned to me and said quietly, 'All right. You can go.' Embarrassed but happy, I put on my warmest clothing and went out into the raging storm. The snowflakes blinded me and the howling wind blew me over more than once. Miraculously, I reached the house, which was actually only a few blocks away, a half an hour later. I rang the bell and then I looked back and saw the shadow of a man walking in the other direction. My father! He had followed me at a distance, never losing sight of me, and watching over every step I took in the storm. That was how much he loved me!"

This story is comparable to the history of the Jews. Because of their resistance to God's Word and commandments, the Lord allowed Israel to leave her house (Jerusalem). She found herself in a violent storm of the world of nations and was led into captivity. However, the God of her fathers followed her and never lost sight of her. He watched over every step she took and brought her home. He will ultimately bring her to His goal for her.

Israel's Plight Without A Shepherd

"Ask ye of the LORD rain in the time of the latter rain; so the LORD shall make bright clouds, and give them showers of rain, to every one grass in the field. For the idols have spoken vanity; and the diviners have seen a lie, and have told false dreams; they comfort in

vain: therefore they went their way as a flock, they were troubled, because there was no shepherd. Mine anger was kindled against the shepherds, and I punished the goats: for the LORD of hosts hath visited his flock the house of Judah, and hath made them as his goodly horse in the battle" (Zechariah 10:1–3). Israel's plight was the result of her seeking help from sources other than the Lord: *"Ask ye of the LORD...the LORD shall make...and give"* (verse 1). All Israel needs, seeks and desires can only be found in God. Besides the literal significance of rain, clouds and grass (verse 1), these words surely have a deeper spiritual significance, for in the context the spiritual restoration of God's people is spoken of. The rain and what it causes to grow is symbolic of blessing, peace and joy, which are the results of the Holy Spirit's outpouring: *"For I will pour water upon him that is thirsty, and floods upon the dry ground: I will pour my spirit upon thy seed, and my blessing upon thine offspring: And they shall spring up as among the grass, as willows by the water courses. One shall say, I am the LORD's; and another shall call himself by the name of Jacob; and another shall subscribe with his hand unto the LORD, and surname himself by the name of Israel"* (Isaiah 44:3–5, also compare to Zechariah 12:10).

It is interesting to note that Zechariah 10:12 says: *"And I will strengthen them in the LORD; and they shall walk up and down in his name, saith the LORD.* " The first and last verses of Zechariah 10 express the past and present inner plight of the Jews. In other words, Israel is hoping for life, peace and rest. However, she does not see that she cannot expect this from America, Europe or the United Nations, but only from God. This problem is very clearly expressed in verse 2. At that time, Israel lent her ear to idols and diviners. Although God had forbidden idolatry and divination in His commandments, she allowed herself to be deceived into doing this by heathen nations. Today Israel is also lending her ear to the nations. Yet up to the present day, nothing has come from this but lies and deception. Israel's hope in the counsel of the nations, and her negotiations with the hostile Palestinian leaders, have ultimately proved to be false. Until now every round of negotiations has turned out to be a *"false dream"* and *"comfort in vain"* (verse 2). Why is this? Because Israel is without a shepherd, *"...therefore they went their way as a flock, they were troubled, because there was no shepherd"* (verse 2).

Israel was taken captive by the Babylonians in 586 B.C. She was in the process of returning during Zechariah's time. She was dispersed among all the nations in 70 A.D. and has been returning ever since the 19th century. Israel has had her own state again with an independent government since the middle of the 20th century (1948). But what she still lacks is the

Good Shepherd. The *"shepherds"* of today's Jews are not leading them in the direction God wants them to go. This refers to the political and religious authorities (rabbis) and it is a tragedy, *"...because there was no shepherd. Mine anger was kindled against the shepherds, and I punished the goats"* (verses 2b and 3). The plight of God's people is said here to be expressly due to the failure of the government at her head. The results are confusion, restlessness, wrong decisions, fear, the entering of the enemies and plundering of the flocks and pastures (chapter 2:12). Israel is back in her own land, but she is still in a state of unbelief towards the Messiah. She has shepherds who cannot help because they turn to God either too seldom, or not at all. Therefore, they do not know how to lead the flock or bring them to rest, so they will ultimately lead Israel into a covenant with the Antichrist.

According to Zechariah 11:16, this false shepherd will come from Israel: *"For, lo, I will raise up a shepherd in the land, which shall not visit those that be cut off, neither shall seek the young one, nor heal that that is broken, nor feed that that standeth still: but he shall eat the flesh of the fat, and tear their claws in pieces."*

Misfortune always occurs when the true Shepherd is missing. We are uprooted and are open to deception. We come into spiritual poverty and restlessness, because the security and safety found in the Good Shepherd are lacking. Every unsaved person is like a lost sheep in need of the Good Shepherd. And any help we seek outside of Him always proves to be unreliable and brings about even more misfortune upon the sheep.

Israel is helpless and insecure because her Good Shepherd has not yet returned. This will change. God is like the father in the story I related in the beginning of this chapter. He is not only following Israel, but He is turning back to her and gathering her under the shepherd's staff of the Messiah.

Israel's Blessing Through The Good Shepherd

"Mine anger was kindled against the shepherds, and I punished the goats: for the LORD of hosts hath visited his flock the house of Judah, and hath made them as his goodly horse in the battle. Out of him came forth the corner, out of him the nail, out of him the battle bow, out of him every oppressor together. And they shall be as mighty men, which tread down their enemies in the mire of the streets in the battle: and they shall fight, because the LORD is with them, and the riders on horses shall be confounded. And I will strengthen the house of Judah, and I will save the house of Joseph, and I will bring them again to place them; for I have mercy upon them: and they shall be as though I had not cast them off: for I am the LORD their God, and will hear them. And they of Ephraim shall be like a mighty man, and their heart shall rejoice

as through wine: yea, their children shall see it, and be glad; their heart shall rejoice in the LORD. I will hiss for them, and gather them; for I have redeemed them: and they shall increase as they have increased" (Zechariah 10:3–8). An inner transformation of the flock will take place when the Lord turns back to His people as the Good Shepherd. Unimagined possibilities will suddenly arise: "...for the LORD of hosts hath visited his flock the house of Judah, and hath made them as his goodly horse in the battle" (chapter 10:3). What a difference! The tousled, straying, lean sheep will become a mighty battle horse!

The cause for this transformation can be found in verse 4: "Out of him came forth the corner, out of him the nail, out of him the battle bow, out of him every oppressor together." Israel's plight was due to those who governed them. Israel's blessing and her inner and outer transformation will be on account of the returning Messiah. The corner, the nail and the battle bow refer to Him.

The "corner" or "cornerstone" (NIV) will come from Judah. It is the Lord Jesus Himself (1st Peter 2:6–8). He was a stumbling stone for Israel at His First Advent. The generation of that time stumbled over Him (Romans 9:32). At His return, He will be the headstone for Israel's ultimate salvation, the culmination of the fulfillment of all the promises God made to her fathers (Zechariah 4:7).

However, Jesus is also the nail or tent-peg (NIV) which provides security and stability to the whole tent. The tent-peg refers to the tabernacle, and the cornerstone to the Temple. The contents—the actual nature of the two buildings—were the glory of the Messiah. He alone is the true stability for the house of Israel. In Him everything will be fulfilled. Isaiah 22:22–23 points to this: *"And the key of the house of David will I lay upon his shoulder; so he shall open, and none shall shut; and he shall shut, and none shall open. And I will fasten him as a nail in a sure place; and he shall be for a glorious throne to his father's house."* Jesus is also the battle bow that will overcome all of Israel's enemies at His return (Revelation 19:11–16). Then every oppressor will have to leave the land, which is what verse 4 probably refers to: *"Out of him every oppressor together…"*

However, this could also be in connection with verse 5, as the NIV translates the last part of this verse as, *"…from him every ruler,"* which would mean that at the beginning of Jesus' reign the powerful men in Israel would be exalted with Him. Personally, I favor the first interpretation.

From Fearful, Persecuted Jews To Heroes

"And they shall be as mighty men, which tread down their enemies in the mire of the streets in the battle: and they shall fight, because the LORD is with

them, and the riders on horses shall be confounded" (verse 5). Historically speaking, this was already fulfilled in the battle of the Maccabees against the Syrians. Through the wars that have taken place in Israel since 1948, it is clearly portrayed that God's Word is not outdated, but is still valid today. In these wars, the Jews who had only recently escaped the Holocaust also suddenly became heroes. This truth will be fulfilled at the last and most violent war at Armageddon. They will not prevail because of their power, their technology, their experience, or their arsenal of weapons. They will be victorious because *"...the Lord is with them."* He is coming Himself as the battle bow at the head of His heavenly armies (Revelation 19). At His return, the powers that previously reigned superior will be leveled. In the wars up until then, He was with them invisibly; but in this last battle He will be seen by every eye.

Israel's Ultimate Gathering

"And I will strengthen the house of Judah, and I will save the house of Joseph, and I will bring them again to place them; for I have mercy upon them: and they shall be as though I had not cast them off: for I am the LORD their God, and will hear them. And they of Ephraim shall be like a mighty man, and their heart shall rejoice as through wine: yea, their children shall see it, and be glad; their heart shall rejoice in the

LORD. *I will hiss for them, and gather them; for I have redeemed them: and they shall increase as they have increased"* (verses 6–8). These verses make it clear that this refers to Israel's ultimate gathering from out of the nations after the Lord has returned, *"...they shall be as though I had not cast them off...and their heart shall rejoice as through wine...for I have redeemed them."* The fruit of this restoration will mean joy in the Lord for Israel's descendants, for they will attain their ultimate redemption. The Lord will call to them like a shepherd calls his flock, in that an angel with a loud trumpet will gather the elect from the four corners of the earth and will lead them back to their homeland (compare to Matthew 24:31 and Isaiah 66:20–23).

The Final Hindrances Are Overcome

"And I will sow them among the people: and they shall remember me in far countries; and they shall live with their children, and turn again. I will bring them again also out of the land of Egypt, and gather them out of Assyria; and I will bring them into the land of Gilead and Lebanon; and place shall not be found for them. And he shall pass through the sea with affliction, and shall smite the waves in the sea, and all the deeps of the river shall dry up: and the pride of Assyria shall be brought down, and the sceptre of Egypt shall depart away. And I will strengthen them in the

LORD; *and they shall walk up and down in his name, saith the LORD"* (Zechariah 10:9–12). When Zechariah wrote these words, the final dispersion of the Jews in 70 A.D. had not yet taken place. For a good hundred years, Israel has been returning from this dispersion to the territories promised them by God. Verse 10 clearly shows that the territory east of the Jordan River (Gilead) and Lebanon belong to Israel. The Good Shepherd will lead them back in such numbers that the land within the present borders will hardly be enough for them. Micah's prayer will find its fulfillment, *"Feed thy people with thy rod, the flock of thine heritage, which dwell solitarily in the wood, in the midst of Carmel: let them feed in Bashan and Gilead, as in the days of old"* (Micah 7:14).

Micah had to wait a long time for the visible answer to this prayer. He died before it came. This is encouraging. The Lord will answer our prayers even if we do not experience it.

Egypt and Syria belong to the last great enemies (verse 10), which are perhaps named synonymously for other world powers. Yet they cannot prevent the Lord from redeeming His people. God uses the picture of Israel's exodus from Egypt through the Red Sea in verse 11 to show us that no power on earth can prevent Him from leading the remnant of His people to their promised inheritance. Daniel 11:40 explains that a terrible war will take place between Egypt, Syria and

Israel, but the Lord will come through as Victor for His people. The Good Shepherd will gather His people beneath His staff and feed them. Then they will attain that which they never attained in the past, *"And I will strengthen them in the LORD; and they shall walk up and down in his name, saith the LORD"* (verse 12).

This chapter can also be of personal significance to us. Perhaps the misfortunes you may have experienced in your life can also be summed up with the words, "You lack the Good Shepherd!" Only through Christ can a much-needed transformation take place in your life. God can make a hero out of a fearful person, a heroine for His kingdom.

Jesus Christ is the God-given stability that every person needs. He offers us the security we cannot find in men. His Cross is the *"cornerstone"* and *"tent-peg"* that anchors us in the kingdom of God. Let Him be your mighty Man, your battle bow who fights for you. Bring your requests to the One who won the victory on Calvary's Cross and through His resurrection.

The Lord is calling you through the signal of His love. He is the Good Shepherd for every lost sheep. He is following you and He is seeking you. Let Him find you! Jesus Christ can overcome every hindrance. He already did it 2,000 years ago, and He is still alive today. No sin in your life is greater than His forgiveness, no fault is greater than His fullness. Call upon

His Name! Then He will say to you, "I will strengthen you in Me, and you will live in My Name."

CHAPTER 15

ISRAEL'S THREE SHEPHERDS

"Open thy doors, O Lebanon, that the fire may devour thy cedars. Howl, fir tree; for the cedar is fallen; because the mighty are spoiled: howl, O ye oaks of Bashan; for the forest of the vintage is come down. There is a voice of the howling of the shepherds; for their glory is spoiled: a voice of the roaring of young lions; for the pride of Jordan is spoiled. Thus saith the LORD my God; Feed the flock of the slaughter; Whose possessors slay them, and hold themselves not guilty: and they that sell them say, Blessed be the LORD; for I am rich: and their own shepherds pity them not. For I will no more pity the inhabitants of the land, saith the LORD: but, lo, I will deliver the men every one into his neighbour's hand, and into the hand of his king: and they shall smite the land, and out of their hand I will not deliver them. And I will feed the flock of slaughter, even you, O poor of the flock. And I took unto me two staves; the one I called Beau-

ty, and the other I called Bands; and I fed the flock. Three shepherds also I cut off in one month; and my soul lothed them, and their soul also abhorred me. Then said I, I will not feed you: that that dieth, let it die; and that that is to be cut off, let it be cut off; and let the rest eat every one the flesh of another. And I took my staff, even Beauty, and cut it asunder, that I might break my covenant which I had made with all the people. And it was broken in that day: and so the poor of the flock that waited upon me knew that it was the word of the LORD. And I said unto them, If ye think good, give me my price; and if not, forbear. So they weighed for my price thirty pieces of silver. And the LORD said unto me, Cast it unto the potter; a goodly price that I was prised at of them. And I took the thirty pieces of silver, and cast them to the potter in the house of the LORD. Then I cut asunder mine other staff, even Bands, that I might break the brotherhood between Judah and Israel. And the LORD said unto me, Take unto thee yet the instruments of a foolish shepherd. For, lo, I will raise up a shepherd in the land, which shall not visit those that be cut off, neither shall seek the young one, nor heal that that is broken, nor feed that that standeth still: but he shall eat the flesh of the fat, and tear their claws in pieces. Woe to the idol shepherd that leaveth the flock! the sword shall be upon his arm, and upon his right eye: his arm shall be clean dried up, and his right eye shall be ut-

terly darkened" (Zechariah 11:1–17).

In this chapter, Israel's Messiah and everything that is connected with Him, leading up to His rejection and the following judgment upon Israel, is described with breathtaking clarity. In the 6th century before Christ, the situation and background as they were at the time of His First Advent are illuminated. The content of Zechariah belongs to the darkest of time periods. It describes the Messiah's rejection and its results. That which Zechariah prophesies in this chapter has been precisely fulfilled according to the Word of God.

The Situation Before The Coming Of Christ

"Open thy doors, O Lebanon, that the fire may devour thy cedars. Howl, fir tree; for the cedar is fallen; because the mighty are spoiled: howl, O ye oaks of Bashan; for the forest of the vintage is come down. There is a voice of the howling of the shepherds; for their glory is spoiled: a voice of the roaring of young lions; for the pride of Jordan is spoiled" (Zechariah 11:1–3). The doors of Lebanon opened for the approaching Roman armies who attacked Israel and occupied her from the north. The Romans left destruction and misery behind them as they made their way through Lebanon. Later on, Jerusalem would also fall, and not one stone of the Temple would remain upon the other. I believe that the words, *"There is a voice of the howling of the shepherds; for their glory is*

spoiled," point to the 70 A.D. destruction of the Temple. For the leaders in Israel, there remained only howling and lamenting. That the cedars fell, the oaks of Bashan and the pride of Jordan were spoiled, could be interpreted to mean that the entire Jewish land and its inhabitants were given over to judgment. Why were they given over to such destruction? The answer was proclaimed almost 600 years before Christ through Zechariah.

It Was The Bad Shepherd's Fault

"Thus saith the LORD my God; Feed the flock of the slaughter; Whose possessors slay them, and hold themselves not guilty: and they that sell them say, Blessed be the LORD; for I am rich: and their own shepherds pity them not. For I will no more pity the inhabitants of the land, saith the LORD: but, lo, I will deliver the men every one into his neighbour's hand, and into the hand of his king: and they shall smite the land, and out of their hand I will not deliver them" (Zechariah 11:4–6). Israel's leaders led the people astray. They didn't behave like shepherds, but like sheep dealers who were only concerned with making a profit. They had no mercy on the flock and impoverished it. They slaughtered the flocks without having to account for their actions. They did what they wanted with the people, and placed an unbearable burden upon them. They were shepherds without mercy who

sought their own glory and wanted to be seen by the people. The "flock of Israel" meant no more to them than sheep for the slaughter. Instead of opening up heaven to them, they closed it. They were blind leaders of the blind.

We need to read the words of judgment Jesus used in Matthew 23 to know just how the leaders really were. But even Jeremiah saw this and described it as follows: *"My people hath been lost sheep: their shepherds have caused them to go astray, they have turned them away on the mountains: they have gone from mountain to hill, they have forgotten their resting-place. All that found them have devoured them: and their adversaries said, We offend not, because they have sinned against the LORD, the habitation of justice, even the LORD, the hope of their fathers"* (Jeremiah 50:6–7, also see Jeremiah 23:1 and Ezekiel 34:2).

When the Lord came to this earth the first time, it was the bad shepherds who instigated His crucifixion: *"But they cried out, Away with him, away with him, crucify him. Pilate saith unto them, Shall I crucify your King? The chief priests answered, We have no king but Caesar"* (John 19:15). In Zechariah 11:6, the Lord said to them, *"For I will no more pity the inhabitants of the land, saith the LORD: but, lo, I will deliver the men every one into his neighbour's hand, and into the hand of his king: and they shall smite the land, and out of their hand I will not deliver them"* (verse 6). They rejected the King of Israel and turned to the Roman emperor, who sent his troops to devastate the land and people in a brutal war. Israel's shepherds — the high priests, elders and scribes — led the people to this catastrophe like lambs to the slaughter.

The Coming Of The Good Shepherd

"And I will feed the flock of slaughter, even you, O poor of the flock. And I took unto me two staves; the one I called Beauty, and the other I called Bands; and I fed the flock. Three shepherds also I cut off in one month; and my soul lothed them, and their soul also abhorred me. Then said I, I will not feed you: that that dieth, let it die; and that that is to be cut off, let it be cut off; and let the rest eat every one the flesh of another. And I took my staff, even Beauty, and cut it asunder, that I might break my covenant which I had made with all the people. And it was broken in that day: and so the poor of the flock that waited upon me knew that it was the word of the LORD. And I said unto them, If ye think good, give me my price; and if not, forbear. So they weighed for my price thirty pieces of silver. And the LORD said unto me, Cast it unto the potter: a goodly price that I was prised at of them. And I took the thirty pieces of silver, and cast them to the potter in the house of the LORD. Then I cut asunder mine other staff, even Bands, that I might break the brotherhood between Judah and Israel" (Zechari-

ah 11:7–14).

The Grace Of God Appeared

"Thus saith the LORD my God; Feed the flock of the slaughter" (verse 4). *"And I will feed the flock of slaughter, even you, O poor of the flock. And I took unto me two staves; the one I called Beauty, and the other I called Bands; and I fed the flock"* (verse 7). A footnote in the Scofield Bible says that the literal translation of the words "Beauty" and "Bands" is "graciousness" and "union." God sent His Son into this situation. In John 10, He referred to Himself as the "Good Shepherd." He came to feed the flock tended by the bad shepherds. He came to draw them to Himself, to unite the divided nation under His rule and to save them. Jesus came in complete graciousness; that is, He came in love and mercy. God's saving grace appeared. He came to bind up the wounded: *"The Spirit of the Lord is upon me, because he hath anointed me to preach the gospel to the poor; he hath sent me to heal the brokenhearted, to preach deliverance to the captives, and recovering of sight to the blind, to set at liberty them that are bruised, To preach the acceptable year of the Lord"* (Luke 4:18–19).

The Rejected One Now Rejects

"Three shepherds also I cut off in one month; and my soul lothed them, and their soul also abhorred me. Then said I, I will not feed you: that that dieth, let it

die; and that that is to be cut off, let it be cut off; and let the rest eat every one the flesh of another" (Zechariah 11:8–9). The high priests, elders and scribes were Israel's three shepherds who rejected the Messiah (Matthew 26:57).

The expression, *"...and their soul also abhorred me,"* expresses a strong dislike to the point of vomiting. The Gospels explain how the Lord rejected the elders and then only spoke in parables. Later, in 70 A.D., they perished. Since then, the Jews have had no priestly shepherds. The Temple, the ephod (part of the priest's garments) and the sacrifices were taken from them (Hosea 3:4–5). But the people also perished with the shepherds. They lost their pasture, the land of Israel. The 70 A.D. siege was so terrible that even cannibalism took place among the people.

The staff called "Beauty" or "Graciousness" is now broken: *"And I took my staff, even Beauty, and cut it asunder, that I might break my covenant which I had made with all the people. And it was broken in that day: and so the poor of the flock that waited upon me knew that it was the word of the LORD"* (Zechariah 11:10–11). With these words, the Lord proclaimed Israel's impending judgment and revealed the possibility of Jerusalem's destruction by the Romans. The staff of graciousness was already broken before the crucifixion of Christ, because He turned away from them before this, and only spoke to them in parables and threatened them with judgment (compare, for example, to Matthew chapters 12, 13 and 23:37–39). Jesus already knew that the leaders of Israel had rejected Him. The staff of graciousness was also broken in verse 10, that is, before the description of betrayal for thirty pieces of silver in verses 12–13. The Gospels confirm this.

After Christ's betrayal and crucifixion, the staff called "Bands" or "Union" was also broken, which in Zechariah also is destroyed only in verse 14 (after the betrayal described in verses 12–13). This is how it was historically. Approximately 37 years following Christ's crucifixion and resurrection, the union in Israel was broken and the land was destroyed by the Romans in 70 A.D.

The covenant with the nations was declared invalid: "...*that I might break my covenant which I had made with all the people.*" I believe that these words prophetically point to the fact that the nations would only be able to attack and overcome Israel with God's permission. This was imminent during Jesus' time. The kingdom was to be taken away from Israel and given to another nation: "*Behold, your house is left unto you desolate*" (Matthew 23:38), and, "... *when ye shall see Jerusalem compassed with armies, then know that the desolation thereof is nigh*" (Luke 21:20).

The elders had already realized that the Lord was applying these words of judgment to them: "*So the covenant was annulled on that day, and thus the most wretched of the flock and the traffickers in the sheep, who were watching me, knew that it was truly the word of the Lord"* (verse 11 — The Amplified Bible). When the Lord told the parable of the householder who had planted a vineyard, and said that the kingdom of God would be taken from them, and that they would be broken and ground to powder by the Stone which the builders rejected, we read: *"And when the chief priests and Pharisees had heard his parables, they perceived that he spake of them"* (Matthew 21:45).

The Official Rejection Of The Messiah

"And I said unto them, If ye think good, give me my price; and if not, forbear. So they weighed for my price thirty pieces of silver. And the LORD said unto me, Cast it unto the potter: a goodly price that I was prised at of them. And I took the thirty pieces of silver, and cast them to the potter in the house of the LORD" (Zechariah 11:12–13). Judas' betrayal of the Lord was foretold with these words. The high priests wanted Jesus out of the way at all costs. Their opportunity came by means of Judas' betrayal. They paid him thirty pieces of silver. The fulfillment of this prophecy is described in Matthew 26:14–15: *"Then one of the twelve, called Judas Iscariot, went unto the chief priests, And said unto them, What will ye give me, and I will deliver him unto you? And they*

covenanted with him for thirty pieces of silver." Remember, Zechariah had already proclaimed this six centuries before Christ was even born. That is a long time before it was actually fulfilled. He was in the same situation as the Son of God had experienced 500 years later.

The background of the thirty pieces of silver is significant. This amount of money was also designated as the amount paid for a slave who was killed by an ox: *"If the ox shall push a manservant or a maidservant; he shall give unto their master thirty shekels of silver"* (Exodus 21:32). The hatred and mockery the high priests had for Jesus is revealed. They hated Him so much that they paid for Him the sum of a killed slave. Jesus was worth nothing to them (Isaiah 53:3).

But Jesus is Jehovah from eternity ("I Am That I Am.") He revealed Himself to His people as Jehovah, but He was of no more value to them than a dead slave. God could not go further in His self-abasement.

"And the LORD said unto me, Cast it unto the potter; a goodly price that I was prised at of them. And I took the thirty pieces of silver, and cast them to the potter in the house of the LORD" (Zechariah 11:13). According to Jewish tradition, a potter was one of the least esteemed workmen during Zechariah's time. If that is the case, this detail, along with the fact that the money was thrown to the potter, makes it even clearer just how despised Jesus was. The money

was not to be thrown just anywhere, however, but *"...to the potter in the house of the Lord."* It would be revealed that Israel had rejected her Messiah in the most holy place. Centuries later, this was fulfilled: *"Then Judas, which had betrayed him, when he saw that he was condemned, repented himself, and brought again the thirty pieces of silver to the chief priests and elders, Saying, I have sinned in that I have betrayed the innocent blood. And they said, What is that to us? see thou to that. And he cast down the pieces of silver in the temple, and departed and went and hanged himself. And the chief priests took the silver pieces, and said, It is not lawful for to put them into the treasury, because it is the price of blood. And they took counsel, and bought with them the potter's field, to bury strangers in"* (Matthew 27:3–7). The phrase, *"...to bury strangers in,"* is really a wonderful fact concealed in the Old Testament. The death of Christ became the salvation of the stranger, that is, the Gentiles, through the rejection on the part of the Jews. They now received the right to take part in Christ's death and resurrection.

The Second Staff Also Broke After Christ's Crucifixion

"Then I cut asunder mine other staff, even Bands (Union), *that I might break the brotherhood between Judah and Israel"* (Zechariah 11:14). We've already seen that prior to Judas' betrayal of Christ, the staff of

"*Graciousness*" had been broken. This pointed to the time when Jesus was among His people and proclaimed judgment to them. The staff of "Union" was broken after Christ's betrayal and crucifixion. Soon after Jesus' ascension, the union between the Jews in the land started to fall apart. Diversion and betrayal took place. Jesus had proclaimed this before in His endtime discourse: "*Now the brother shall betray the brother to death, and the father the son; and children shall rise up against their parents, and shall cause them to be put to death*" (Mark 13:12). "*And then shall many be offended, and shall betray one another, and shall hate one another*" (Matthew 24:10). This came to pass in 70 A.D. The Romans attacked Jerusalem, destroyed everything, and the Jews were dispersed all over the world. The union which had previously held everything together was now gone.

The Coming Of The Bad Shepherd

"*And the LORD said unto me, Take unto thee yet the instruments of a foolish shepherd. For, lo, I will raise up a shepherd in the land, which shall not visit those that be cut off, neither shall seek the young one, nor heal that that is broken, nor feed that that standeth still: but he shall eat the flesh of the fat, and tear their claws in pieces. Woe to the idol shepherd that leaveth the flock! the sword shall be upon his arm, and upon his right eye: his arm shall be clean dried up, and his right eye shall be utterly darkened"* (Zechariah 11:15–17). Just as Jesus' endtime discourse on the Mount of Olives contains a double meaning (the first fulfillment in 70 A.D. and the main fulfillment in the coming Great Tribulation), so too does Zechariah 11 link the events at the time of Christ on earth to the endtimes. Israel's situation at Christ's First Advent included the rejection of the Messiah, the destruction of Jerusalem and the razing of the land by the Romans. Now we are led to the endtimes.

The Bad Shepherd's Proclamation

Zechariah had to play the part of a bad shepherd: *"And the LORD said unto me, Take unto thee yet the instruments of a foolish shepherd"* (verse 15). This foolish shepherd personifies the false Messiah, the Antichrist, the man of sin and the son of perdition (2nd Thessalonians 2). He doesn't come to feed Israel, but he comes to rob her.

Jesus spoke of him in John 10:10–11: *"The thief cometh not, but for to steal, and to kill, and to destroy: I am come that they might have life, and that they might have it more abundantly. I am the good shepherd: the good shepherd giveth his life for the sheep."* But because the Jews rejected the Good Shepherd, the bad shepherd would now come in His place. The Lord also foretold this: *"I am come in my Father's name, and ye receive me not: if another shall come in his own name, him ye will receive"* (John 5:43).

The Bad Shepherd's Appearance

"For, lo, I will raise up a shepherd in the land, which shall not visit those that be cut off, neither shall seek the young one, nor heal that that is broken, nor feed that that standeth still: but he shall eat the flesh of the fat, and tear their claws in pieces" (Zechariah 11:16). Like Jesus, the Antichrist will appear "in the land" – *Eretz Israel*. I believe that he is the second beast introduced in Revelation 13:11 and following who comes up from out of the earth, in contrast to the first beast who comes from out of the sea. The land is symbolic of Israel and the sea represents the nations. This beast will bring terrible destruction upon Israel and all who believe in Jesus. He will kill those who do not worship the image of the first beast (Revelation 13:15).

It is striking that the evil shepherd does the exact opposite of that which the Lord did as the Good Shepherd. Jesus said, *"The Spirit of the Lord is upon me, because he hath anointed me to preach the gospel to the poor; he hath sent me to heal the brokenhearted, to preach deliverance to the captives, and recovering of sight to the blind, to set at liberty them that are bruised, To preach the acceptable year of the Lord"* (Luke 4:18–19). In contrast to this, it says of the bad shepherd: *"...which shall not visit those that be cut* off, *neither shall seek the young one, nor heal that that is broken, nor feed that that standeth still: but he shall eat the flesh of the fat, and tear their claws in pieces"* (Zechariah 11:16).

The Bad Shepherd's End

"Woe to the idol shepherd that leaveth the flock! the sword shall be upon his arm, and upon his right eye: his arm shall be clean dried up, and his right eye shall be utterly darkened" (Zechariah 11:17). According to Jewish tradition, the arm is a sign of power and the right eye a sign of intelligence. We know from the book of Daniel that the Antichrist will appear on the scene with the utmost devilish intelligence and power.

A prophetic example of this is found in Daniel 8: *"And in the latter time of their kingdom, when the transgressors are come to the full, a king of fierce countenance, and understanding dark sentences* ("a master of intrigue" – NIV), *shall stand up. And his power shall be mighty, but not by his own power: and he shall destroy wonderfully, and shall prosper, and practise, and shall destroy the mighty and the holy people. And through his policy also he shall cause craft to prosper in his hand; and he shall magnify himself in his heart, and by peace shall destroy many: he shall also stand up against the Prince of princes; but he shall be broken without hand"* (Daniel 8:23–25). At that time, this referred to Antiochus Epiphanes, but it also applies to the Antichrist of the endtimes. At the end of days, the Lord will return and make an end to the Antichrist. He will destroy him with the breath of his mouth (2nd Thessalonians 2). Then the Lord Himself will return for Israel as the Good Shepherd: *"Behold, the Lord GOD will come with strong hand, and his arm shall rule for him: behold, his reward is with him, and his work before him. He shall feed his flock like a shepherd: he shall gather the lambs with his arm, and carry them in his bosom, and shall gently lead those that are with young"* (Isaiah 40:10–11).

CHAPTER 16

JERUSALEM: CUP OF TREMBLING, BURDENSOME STONE AND HEARTH OF FIRE

"The burden of the word of the LORD for Israel, saith the LORD, which stretcheth forth the heavens, and layeth the foundation of the earth, and formeth the spirit of man within him. Behold, I will make Jerusalem a cup of trembling unto all the people round about, when they shall be in the siege both against Judah and against Jerusalem. And in that day will I make Jerusalem a burdensome stone for all people: all that burden themselves with it shall be cut in pieces, though all the people of the earth be gathered together against it. In that day, saith the LORD, I will smite every horse with astonishment, and his rider with madness: and I will open mine eyes upon the house of Judah, and will smite every horse of the people with blindness. And the governors of Judah shall say in their heart, The inhabitants of Jerusalem shall be my

strength in the LORD of hosts their God. In that day will I make the governors of Judah like an hearth of fire among the wood, and like a torch of fire in a sheaf; and they shall devour all the people round about, on the right hand and on the left: and Jerusalem shall be inhabited again in her own place, even in Jerusalem. The LORD also shall save the tents of Judah first, that the glory of the house of David and the glory of the inhabitants of Jerusalem do not magnify themselves against Judah. In that day shall the LORD defend the inhabitants of Jerusalem; and he that is feeble among them at that day shall be as David; and the house of David shall be as God, as the angel of the LORD before them. And it shall come to pass in that day, that I will seek to destroy all the nations that come against Jerusalem" (Zechariah 12:1–9).

Jerusalem is mentioned nine times in this passage. The words "people" or "nations" occur six times. Zechariah 12 clearly describes the endtimes (verse 8). The nations will increasingly focus upon Jerusalem in the last days. A recent advertisement in a Swiss newspaper said: "The most important bookmark of Switzerland. Jerusalem, Peking, Washington...our editors will keep you informed from morning to night *on the most* important developments." Notice how Jerusalem is listed even before world capitals such as Peking and Washington. This is typical of our time. The eyes and thoughts of the nation remain on Jerusalem, a city that has become a daily topic of conversation in the media. For world politicians, she is at the top of the list of political themes. To the Arab world, Jerusalem remains its greatest bone of contention. This is why Jerusalem is also a great religious theme.

Jerusalem has evolved from a political point of discussion to a major offense that must be resolved. Jerusalem is that cup of trembling and burdensome stone for the nations. The city is becoming a more delicate and complex issue. She is the target of the nations' hatred for the God of Israel.

The Prologue Of The God Of Israel

"The burden of the word of the LORD for Israel, saith the LORD, which stretcheth forth the heavens, and layeth the foundation of the earth, and formeth the spirit of man within him" (Zechariah 12:1).

Zechariah 12:1 serves as a tremendous prologue by God on the subject of Israel. In fact, you could even say that it is a prologue to the last stage of Jerusalem's history. Better words could not have been chosen to give this theme the significance it holds for God. The same God Who created heaven and earth, Who gave man His spirit (breath) (Genesis 2:7) at creation, Who spoke the first word in world history even before man existed, this same God will also have the last word concerning Jerusalem. The first verse says that this message comes from God Himself. In its battle over

Jerusalem, the world is dealing with Almighty God, the Creator. God's sovereign power is so great that it embraces all things — heaven and earth. Man has a spirit (the breath of God) that enables him to seek God, read His Word and act upon it. This spirit in the heart of man is aimed at God. These words are directed to Israel. This is a mighty comfort in view of Jerusalem's future. Throughout all the crises, Jerusalem will become what God has destined for her.

Jerusalem – A Cup Of Trembling For The Islamic Nations

"Behold, I will make Jerusalem a cup of trembling unto all the people round about, when they shall be in the siege both against Judah and against Jerusalem" (Zechariah 12:2, also compare to Ezekiel 28:26). Although Zechariah lived in the 6th century before Christ, and Islam wasn't introduced until the 7th century after Christ's death, the prophet already saw an endtime problem between Islam and Judaism. The nations surrounding Jerusalem are Islamic. Israel is like a tiny oasis in the middle of a gigantic Arab-Islamic world. This is why she is called a "cancer" by most Arab nations. Achmed Shukeiri, one of the PLO leaders said, "Zionism is worse than Fascism, more evil than Nazism, more despicable than Imperialism and more dangerous than Colonialism. Zionism is a concentration of all these evils. It must be destroyed."

Jerusalem is a cup of trembling for the Islamic extremists. The *Sharia* (interpretation of Islamic law) forbids the consumption of alcohol, yet the Muslims seem to be intoxicated where Jerusalem is concerned. They are drunk over Jerusalem. A drunk man usually feels stronger than he actually is; he can no longer assess a situation realistically. He becomes boastful and careless. In his intoxicated state of mind, he says things he wouldn't say if he were sober because they are not factual and would not stand up against proper examination.

The goal of all Islamic terror groups is the destruction of the Jews. Their Palestinian state must replace Israel. Sheich Achmed Yassin, chief of the Hamas movement, said, "The earth of Palestine is an Islamic sanctuary which belongs to the Muslims to the end of time. The liberation of all Palestine, from the sea to the river (Jordan) is the highest strategic goal."

The behavior of many Islamic fundamentalists is so irrational that even the Jordanian newspaper, *The Jordan Times,* made the following statement: "Six million Israelis live on our border, and whether we like it or not, we cannot ignore what they think and how they see the regional developments, what they fear and what they are aiming at." *The Jordan Times* criticized the continual ignorance of Arab intellectuals and the arrogance of Arab students who did not deem it necessary to find out more about the Israeli society. "This is stupidity and dangerous nearsightedness."

There will be a future warlike confrontation between Islam and Judaism. *The Jordan Times* wrote, "The Israeli society is like a ship in the midst of the storm of the Israeli-Arab conflict, which can be shattered at any moment."

What Could This War Look Like?

"Behold, I will make Jerusalem a cup of trembling unto all the people round about, when they shall be in the siege both against Judah and against Jerusalem" (verse 2). The war could begin in Judah when Jerusalem is attacked by the Arab nations. On one hand, this would be a war from the outside, but on the other hand, it would also be a war from within. Zechariah 14:14 says, *"And Judah also shall fight at Jerusalem."* Many Arabs live in Judaea, in contrast to Jerusalem, which is mainly inhabited by Jews. The Palestinian police force has a strength of at least 30-50,000 men today. The National Security Powers (NSE), employed to watch over the borders of the autonomous territories, have a strength of roughly 14,000 men. The PLO bodyguards comprise approximately 3,000 men. The Security Service (PSF) is made up of 5,000 plainclothes agents. The official news service Muchabarat al Umma, responsible for the news service and counter-espionage, comprises approximately 3,000 employees. When Israel is attacked from

the outside, it could happen that a threat to Israel could come from within the territory of Judah.

Jerusalem – A Burdensome Stone For All Nations

"And in that day will I make Jerusalem a burdensome stone for all people: all that burden themselves with it shall be cut in pieces, though all the people of the earth be gathered together against it" (Zechariah 12:3). This is a gloomy prophetic picture of Jerusalem's future. According to this statement, all discussions over Jerusalem — the endless negotiations, the futile search for peace, any effort that continually ends in failure — will turn into pure hatred. Then only one option will remain: Jerusalem must be eradicated. This city will become a burdensome stone. But this idea is destined to fail because Jerusalem is like a rough stone with sharp contours that injure those who try to remove it.

The Satan-led nations will seek to eradicate the location of God's revelation. Satan sought to seat himself on God's throne in heaven. Subsequently, he was banished (Isaiah 14:13–14 and Ezekiel 28:2:17). Now he wants to sit on the throne in Jerusalem, but this throne is only intended for the Messiah (Jeremiah 3:17). So Satan wants to destroy Jerusalem; he wants to prevent the throne of God from being established in Jerusalem at all costs.

The prophecy shows that the conflict with the Arab

nations will spread to all the other nations. Even today we see more clearly that the nations of the world are being drawn into the Israel-Palestinian conflict. But the united attempt to eradicate Jerusalem will be to the detriment of the nations.

Judah: A Hearth Of Fire For All Nations

"In that day will I make the governors of Judah like an hearth of fire among the wood, and like a torch of fire in a sheaf; and they shall devour all the people round about, on the right hand and on the left: and Jerusalem shall be inhabited again in her own place, even in Jerusalem" (verse 6). In reaction to the boycott of Jerusalem's 3,000-year celebration by various nations, including the European Union and the United Nations, Jerusalem's mayor Ehud Olmert said the following:

"Jerusalem was Israel's capital long before you existed. And she will be Israel's undivided capital long after your protests have disappeared and only to be found in history books!"

Jerusalem is not only turning into a delicate subject for the world, but she is becoming God's *"hearth of fire"* against the nations. Something is about to happen. The nations will begin to feel very strong and superior and will unite their military strength against Jerusalem. What will happen? What does a torch do to straw? One lit matchstick is enough to make straw burn. Imagine what a torch would do! The nations will desire to eradicate Israel, but instead, they will burn. Wood and straw will be burned, but Jerusalem will remain. She cannot be removed or destroyed because she has an eternally valid destiny. Jerusalem is the city of the great King!

The power of the Jews lies in God and His promises. Israel will not be victorious over her enemies through her own power or military strength, but through the God who created heaven and earth: *"In that day, saith the LORD, I will smite every horse with astonishment, and his rider with madness: and I will open mine eyes upon the house of Judah, and will smite every horse of the people with blindness"* (Zechariah 12:4).

The God of Israel does not let His people out of His sight. He describes them as the *"apple of His eye"* (chapter 2:12), and He will fight against the enemies of His people: *"And the governors of Judah shall say in their heart, The inhabitants of Jerusalem shall be my strength in the LORD of hosts their God"* (verse 5). In the midst of this war, the Jews will begin to trust in God more and more, and they will encourage one another, not with political speeches, but with the powerful Word of God.

These are the signs of a revival in Israel: *"The LORD also shall save the tents of Judah first, that the glory of the house of David and the glory of the in-*

habitants of Jerusalem do not magnify themselves against Judah" (verse 7). The Judaeans will need help when Islamic fundamentalist enemies from the midst of Judah start fighting against Israel. The Lord will come to the aid of the Jews in Judaea. Through this, a certain disagreement between Jerusalem and Judah will be removed and a union will come about. Judaea will become a hearth of fire for the nations because of God's intervention. The people of Jerusalem will be encouraged and strengthened: *"In that day shall the LORD defend the inhabitants of Jerusalem; and he that is feeble among them at that day shall be as David; and the house of David shall be as God, as the angel of the LORD before them"* (verse 8).

The comparisons are breathtaking: God's intervention and protection on Israel's behalf will cause miracles to take place, so that even the weakest in Jerusalem will be like David in his battle against Goliath. The house of David will be like God Himself, like the angel of the Lord (Jesus) who went ahead of them, protecting them as they wandered through the wilderness. *"And it shall come to pass in that day, that I will seek to destroy all the nations that come against Jerusalem"* (verse 9). It cannot be made any clearer how God sees Jerusalem and how He judges people where their dealings with Jerusalem are concerned.

Jerusalem's cup of trembling will drive the nations mad. They will seek to become intoxicated, but they will be poisoned. The cup of trembling will become a cup of God's wrath for all of Israel's enemies: *"For thus saith the LORD God of Israel unto me; Take the wine cup of this fury at my hand, and cause all the nations, to whom I send thee, to drink it. And they shall drink, and be moved, and be mad, because of the sword that I will send among them"* (Jeremiah 25:15–16).

Let's summarize: The enemies want to remove the burdensome stone of Jerusalem, but they will cut themselves on it. Those who attack Israel will themselves be burned. However, Jerusalem will remain where she is because God's promises stand forever: *"And thine house and thy kingdom shall be established for ever before thee: thy throne shall be established for ever"* (2nd Samuel 7:16); *"For thus saith the LORD; David shall never want a man to sit upon the throne of the house of Israel"* (Jeremiah 33:17). This will find its complete fulfillment in the Lord Jesus Christ!

CHAPTER 17

THE REVELATION OF THE SON OF GOD

*"And I will pour upon the house of David, and up-
on the inhabitants of Jerusalem, the spirit of grace and
of supplications: and they shall look upon me whom
they have pierced, and they shall mourn for him, as
one mourneth for his only son, and shall be in bitterness for him, as one that is in bitterness for his firstborn. In that day shall there be a great mourning in
Jerusalem, as the mourning of Hadadrimmon in the
valley of Megiddon. And the land shall mourn, every
family apart; The family of the house of David apart,
and their wives apart; the family of the house of
Nathan apart, and their wives apart; the family of the
house of Levi apart, and their wives apart; the family
of Shimei apart, and their wives apart; All the families
that remain, every family apart, and their wives apart"*
(Zechariah 12:10–14).

It is a wonderful thing when God the Father draws
a person to His Son, Jesus Christ, when He opens our

eyes and gives us the grace to fully repent. A young man who grew up in a Christian home once said, "I used to read the Bible out of a sense of duty. I thought that God would punish me if I didn't. But I never wanted to be converted. I could not, and did not, want to let go of the world. I led a somewhat confused life. One day I sat in a church service and was suddenly so deeply moved, I saw my lost life and began to weep. I repented of my sins and was converted. Suddenly everything was different. I only noticed later on that I did not do certain things any more that had always been quite normal for me before. Today, Jesus is the greatest and most important person to me."

What happened to this young man? The Holy Spirit came into his life and led him to Jesus. This man's eyes were opened and he was led out of his spiritual blindness. The entire nation of Israel will experience this same type of conversion. As they are awakened by the Spirit of God, their blindness will be removed, they will recognize Jesus as the Son of God, and they will repent. This will be a national conversion of the Jewish people (2nd Corinthians 3:16). These five verses impressively describe how God will do this. They serve as strong evidence that God has not given up on His people.

The Great Turning Point

The turning point will come in the midst of the

Jews' greatest distress. All the nations will march against Israel and attack. The last verse of the preceding passage says, *"And it shall come to pass in that day, that I will seek to destroy all the nations that come against Jerusalem"* (Zechariah 12:9). The Lord's power is demonstrated in His wrath toward the armies that are hostile toward Israel. But the power of God's grace is demonstrated in the salvation of the Jews. It will not be the outward distress of the Great Tribulation that will lead Israel to the inward turning point; that will be accomplished by the inner working of the Holy Spirit: *"And I will pour upon the house of David, and upon the inhabitants of Jerusalem, the spirit of grace and of supplications"* (verse 10). If God didn't do this, Israel would never return to the Lord. But God will do it because He has promised to do it, and He is looking at His Son. Israel must recognize the Son of God, but this can only take place through the Spirit of God.

When Jesus celebrated the Last Supper with His disciples, He introduced a New Covenant, the New Testament, in His blood (see Matthew 26:28; Mark 14:24; Luke 22:20 and 1st Corinthians 11:25). This covenant is founded on the work of redemption in Jesus, but it is effective through the Spirit of God. The Jewish people are being led toward this New Covenant, which was even proclaimed by the prophets.

Read the following verses:

- *"And I will give them one heart, and I will put a new spirit within you; and I will take the stony heart out of their flesh, and will give them an heart of flesh: That they may walk in my statutes, and keep mine ordinances, and do them: and they shall be my people, and I will be their God"* (Ezekiel 11:19–20, also compare to Ezekiel 36:27 and 37:14).

- *"And so all Israel shall be saved: as it is written, There shall come out of Sion the Deliverer, and shall turn away ungodliness from Jacob: For this is my covenant unto them, when I shall take away their sins"* (Romans 11:26–27).

- *"Moreover I will make a covenant of peace with them; it shall be an everlasting covenant with them: and I will place them, and multiply them, and will set my sanctuary in the midst of them forevermore"* (Ezekiel 37:26).

- *"For finding fault with them, he saith, Behold, the days come, saith the Lord, when I will make a new covenant with the house of Israel and with the house of Judah: Not according to the covenant that I made with their fathers in the day when I took them by the hand to lead them out of the land of Egypt; because they continued not in my covenant, and I regarded them not, saith the Lord. For this is the covenant that I will make with the house of Israel after those days, saith the Lord; I will put my laws into their mind, and write them in their hearts: and I will be to them a God, and they shall be to me a people: And they shall not teach every man his neighbour, and every man his brother, saying, Know the Lord: for all shall know me, from the least to the greatest"* (Hebrews 8:8–11).

Under the Old Covenant, which was founded on the Law given at Sinai, God said, *"If you...you will"* (Exodus 19:5). Under the New Covenant it says, *"I will"* (Hebrews 8:10, 12). Under the Old Covenant, obedience came out of fear, but under the New Covenant, obedience comes from the Spirit who gives a willing heart. This covenant will produce supplication and corresponding grace in Israel. The grace of the Holy Spirit will lead them to the crucified Savior: *"...they shall look upon me whom they have pierced"* (Zechariah 12:10).

The Jews will not be led to salvation by passing by the Cross, but by heading straight for it. The people who have ignored Him for centuries by purposely passing over Isaiah 53 and other Messianic passages in their synagogues will be led to Calvary, for there, salvation was wrought for them. At Calvary, that which Moses pointed to prophetically in the wilderness when he lifted up the brass serpent will become clear. The Israelites had sinned grievously at that time; they were impatient and spoke out against God, complaining and despising the food He provided for them. Then the Lord had sent poisonous serpents, some of which had bitten the Israelites, causing many to die. The Israelites saw the tragedy and results of their sins and cried out, *"We have sinned…"*. Moses prayed to God on behalf of his people, and God instructed Moses to lift up a brass serpent. Everyone who had been bitten by a serpent could look to the serpent Moses had erected and be saved: *"And Moses made a serpent of brass, and put it upon a pole, and it came to pass, that if a serpent had bitten any man, when he beheld the serpent of brass, he lived"* (Numbers 21:9).

The Bible casts a prophetic light on the history of the Jews at Jesus' First Advent. They became impatient with Jesus; they were annoyed with Him and spoke out against Him. The Jews despised Him as the Bread of Life God had sent. The results were devastating. Many of the Jewish people died as a result of this rejection. However, Jesus is simultaneously the exalted serpent. He was made to be sin for us and subsequently wrought forgiveness and salvation for us. Thus, the Lord referred to this story in the wilderness, saying, *"And as Moses lifted up the serpent in the wilderness, even so must the Son of man be lifted up: That whosoever believeth in him should not perish, but have eternal life. For God so loved the world, that he gave his only begotten Son, that whosoever believeth in him should not perish, but have everlasting life"* (John 3:14–16). The remnant of Israel is being led toward this point. Israel will look upon the Cross of

Calvary, acknowledging the One whom they had pierced, and will find their redemption.

The story of the crucifixion makes clear the fact that Jesus died for the Jews, and that they will partake of this accomplished salvation: *"But when they came to Jesus, and saw that he was dead already, they brake not his legs: But one of the soldiers with a spear pierced his side, and forthwith came there out blood and water. And he that saw it bare record, and his record is true: and he knoweth that he saith true, that ye might believe. For these things were done, that the scripture should be fulfilled, A bone of him shall not be broken. And again another scripture saith, They shall look on him whom they pierced"* (John 19:33–37).

At that time, a centuries-old prophecy was fulfilled, but they did not recognize it. Because God knew this already, the Holy Spirit referred to another text and testified for Israel's future: *"They shall look on him whom they pierced."* A time span of 2000 year lies between these two statements.

When the Lord returns, that will take place which is described here, for Revelation 1:7 says, *"Behold, he cometh with clouds; and every eye shall see him, and they also which pierced him: and all kindreds of the earth shall wail because of him. Even so, Amen."* This verse could also be translated as, "All the tribes of the land shall wail because of him."

Recognition Of The Son Of God

"And they shall mourn for him, as one mourneth for his only son, and shall be in bitterness for him, as one that is in bitterness for his firstborn" (Zechariah 12:10). At their conversion, the Jews will not only recognize their Messiah, the promised Redeemer, the crucified One, but they will also recognize the Son of God and Son of man. This means nothing other than that they will find in Jesus true God and true Man. They will weep over Him as one weeps over an only son. Jesus, the only-begotten Son of God, is also the only true Son of Israel, produced by the Jewish people.

Certainly the Lord did not only connect the two without a reason when He spoke about the raised serpent. There He spoke about the Son of man, who comes from the line of Israel, but also about the Son of God, who comes from heaven. Jesus makes it clear that He is both: *"And as Moses lifted up the serpent in the wilderness, even so must the Son of man be lifted up"* (John 3:14). And then, *"For God so loved the world, that he gave his only begotten Son, that whosoever believeth in him should not perish, but have everlasting life"* (John 3:16).

Jesus is the one of whom Daniel spoke of in Daniel 7:13–14: *"I saw in the night visions, and, behold, one like the Son of man came with the clouds of heaven, and came to the Ancient of days, and they brought him near before him. And there was given him do-*

minion, and glory, and a kingdom, that all people, na-
tions, and languages, should serve him: his dominion
is an everlasting dominion, which shall not pass away,
and his kingdom that which shall not be destroyed."
When Israel sees Him as the pierced One, as the One
who hung upon the Cross, she will recognize Him as
both and will weep over Him and repent. Israel will
lament over Him as the One and Only Son whom she
has lost, for she will see that God came to her in Jesus,
but that she rejected Him at His First Advent
(Zechariah 14:9).

Israel's National Repentance

This knowledge will lead Israel to a deep repentance
that she has never experienced in her entire history.

Jerusalem

"In that day shall there be a great mourning in
Jerusalem, as the mourning of Hadadrimmon in the
valley of Megiddon" (Zechariah 12:11). Israel's Lord
was crucified in Jerusalem. The people of Jerusalem
cried, *"Away with him...we do not want this man to*
reign over us...His blood be on us, and on our chil-
dren!" They mocked Him, smote their breasts at His
crucifixion and returned to their daily routines. This is
why Jerusalem's repentance is mentioned first. It is
compared to Israel's lamenting in Hadadrimmon in
the valley of Megiddon. Perhaps the Bible is referring
to Jeremiah's lamentation when the God-fearing King

Josiah was killed in the valley of Megiddon (2nd Chronicles 35:20–25).

The Land

"*And the land shall mourn, every family apart*" (Zechariah 12:12). At that time, Jesus traveled throughout the land, and so the entire land will repent and will receive forgiveness. Jesus' ministry will not remain barren: "*I will remove the iniquity of that land in one day*" (Zechariah 3:9).

Every Family For Itself

"*All the families that remain, every family apart, and their wives apart*" (Zechariah 12:14). Verses 12-14 emphasize that no family is left out. Women and men will repent separately and lament, just as today women and men are separated in the synagogues and at the Wailing Wall. When the Lord was crucified, it says, "*And all the people that came together to that sight, beholding the things which were done, smote their breasts, and returned*" (Luke 23:48). The masses in Israel will repent when Jesus returns.

The Family Of David

"*The family of the house of David apart, and their wives apart*" (Zechariah 12:12). King David sinned grievously against the Lord — now the house of David will repent. Surely this is a pointer to Israel's political leadership.

The Family Of Nathan

"*The family of the house of Nathan apart, and their wives apart*" (Zechariah 12:12). Nathan was the prophet who had rebuked David after his fall into sin and led him back to God. Yet even this prophetic family will repent — a picture of the Old Testament prophets.

The Family Of Levi

"*The family of the house of Levi apart, and their wives apart*" (Zechariah 12:13). Levi is the priestly tribe that which brought the offerings. From this tribe came the high priest who led the great Day of Atonement. It was the religious authorities who persecuted and accused Jesus, and ultimately had Him condemned to death through Pilate. They will also repent.

The Family Of Shimei

"*The family of Shimei apart, and their wives apart*" (Zechariah 12:13). Shimei came from the house of Saul. He cursed David when the latter was fleeing from Absalom, threw stones at him and called him "*a bloody man*" (2nd Samuel 16:5–14). This family will also repent. Perhaps this refers to the restoration of the house of Saul.

This list of names represents all the classes of the house of Israel and the whole Jewish population. Nobody is excluded. This points to Romans 11:26: "*And so all Israel shall be saved: as it is written, There shall come out of Sion the Deliverer, and shall turn away ungodliness from Jacob."*

In this portrayal of repentance lies a deep, earnest truth: No person can repent for another. Everyone must come to God personally. God has no grandchildren. Without repentance and a turning to Jesus Christ, there is no way into the kingdom of God. Everyone must repent personally and be converted. It does not matter whether or not you have had a Christian upbringing, whether you go to a Christian church, or whether you take part in Christian activities. Whoever does not come to Jesus with all his heart cannot be saved. This was how it was in the Old Testament. Nobody could look at the brass serpent for another. Each person had to do it for himself if he wanted to live.

CHAPTER 18

ISRAEL'S SPIRITUAL RENEWAL

"In that day there shall be a fountain opened to the house of David and to the inhabitants of Jerusalem for sin and for uncleanness. And it shall come to pass in that day, saith the LORD of hosts, that I will cut off the names of the idols out of the land, and they shall no more be remembered: and also I will cause the prophets and the unclean spirit to pass out of the land. And it shall come to pass, that when any shall yet prophesy, then his father and his mother that begat him shall say unto him, Thou shalt not live; for thou speakest lies in the name of the LORD: and his father and his mother that begat him shall thrust him through when he prophesieth. And it shall come to pass in that day, that the prophets shall be ashamed every one of his vision, when he hath prophesied; neither shall they wear a rough garment to deceive: But he shall say, I am no prophet, I am an husbandman; for man taught me to keep cattle from my youth. And

257

one shall say unto him, What are these wounds in thine hands? Then he shall answer, Those with which I was wounded in the house of my friends. Awake, O sword, against my shepherd, and against the man that is my fellow, saith the LORD of hosts: smite the shepherd, and the sheep shall be scattered: and I will turn mine hand upon the little ones. And it shall come to pass, that in all the land, saith the LORD, two parts therein shall be cut off and die; but the third shall be left therein. And I will bring the third part through the fire, and will refine them as silver is refined, and will try them as gold is tried: they shall call on my name, and I will hear them: I will say, It is my people: and they shall say, The LORD is my God" (Zechariah 13:1–9).

The last three chapters of the book of Zechariah deal with the great subject of the events of the end-times in Israel that are directly connected with Jesus' return. Therefore, the descriptions in chapters 12–14 are intertwined.

The main topic is the "Day of the Lord"—the events of the Great Tribulation. The little phrase *"in that day"* continually occurs in these three chapters, making it clear that we are concerned here with a single theme (Zechariah 12;3, 4, 6, 8a, 8b, 9 and 11, 13:1 and 4 and 14:4,6,8,9,13,20 and 21.)

The Consequences Of Repentance

"In that day there shall be a fountain opened to the

house of David and to the inhabitants of Jerusalem for sin and for uncleanness" (Zechariah 13:1). This verse directly follows the events of chapter 12:10–14. Israel looks upon Him whom she has pierced, the spirit of grace is poured out and her blindness is removed. Through this, Israel recognizes in Jesus the rejected Messiah, the Son of God and the Son of man.

This is followed by a sincere movement of repentance through all classes in Israel, and the consequences are immediate forgiveness and streams of living water. The magnitude of Jesus' sacrifice demands nothing of us but sincere repentance. No further conditions and forgiveness follow repentance.

David, whose family is mentioned here, is a wonderful example of this. When the king of Israel sinned grievously against God through carelessness, adultery and instigation to murder, he was convicted through the prophet Nathan. Then David realized the tragedy of his sin and repented, and this repentance was followed by immediate forgiveness: *"And David said unto Nathan, I have sinned against the LORD. And Nathan said unto David, The LORD also hath put away thy sin; thou shalt not die"* (2nd Samuel 12:13).

God's forgiveness is not merely a single event, but it is continual. This means that forgiveness is a power which should have continual influence in our lives. It is there to liberate us from all bondage and contamination. It is a fountain open for every sin and defilement. Forgiveness contains an enduring power as it proceeds from a fountain. From these streams of living water come continual renewal of life. This is why the psalmist prayed, *"For with thee is the fountain of life"* (Psalm 36:9).

This fountain of forgiveness and life comes from the hill of Calvary, where Jesus shed His blood for the forgiveness of sins. After He died, *"...one of the soldiers with a spear pierced his side, and forthwith came there out blood and water"* (John 19:34).

The people and land of Israel will enter into a state of complete redemption. This is made clear in the picture of Joshua the high priest: *"And he* (the angel of the Lord) *answered and spake unto those that stood before him, saying, Take away the filthy garments from him. And unto him he said, Behold, I have caused thine iniquity to pass from thee, and I will clothe thee with change of raiment"* (Zechariah 3:4), and *"I* (the Lord of hosts) *will remove the iniquity of that land in one day"* (Zechariah 3:9).

The New Testament also speaks of Israel's future forgiveness, the foundation of which was laid at Calvary: *"And so all Israel shall be saved: as it is written, There shall come out of Sion the Deliverer, and shall turn away ungodliness from Jacob"* (Romans 11:26).

The Consequences Of True Conversion

The consequences of true conversion include the

complete reign of Jesus in Israel's life, thus the practical turning away from all sins. This is also true in our lives. *"And it shall come to pass in that day, saith the LORD of hosts, that I will cut off the names of the idols out of the land, and they shall no more be remembered: and also I will cause the prophets and the unclean spirit to pass out of the land. And it shall come to pass, that when any shall yet prophesy, then his father and his mother that begat him shall say unto him, Thou shalt not live; for thou speakest lies in the name of the LORD: and his father and his mother that begat him shall thrust him through when he prophesieth. And it shall come to pass in that day, that the prophets shall be ashamed every one of his vision, when he hath prophesied; neither shall they wear a rough garment to deceive: But he shall say, I am no prophet, I am an husbandman; for man taught me to keep cattle from my youth"* (Zechariah 13:2–6). Since Israel's return to the Promised Land, idolatry, and consequently a spirit of impurity, have spread. Israel has become a center for many religions, which are all tolerated by the Jewish state. For instance, in Haifa, there is a gigantic garden of the Bahai religion. It is the world center of this religion. In Jerusalem and throughout the land, are countless churches and monuments of the Greek Orthodox and Roman Catholic churches. And on the Dome of the Rock now stands where the house of the Lord once stood. However, the climax of all idolatry will be set up by the Antichrist when he establishes the abomination of desolation in the holy place (Matthew 24:15 and 2nd Thessalonians 2:3–4). When Jesus returns to set up His kingdom in Israel, He will first remove this abomination. Daniel speaks of this: *"And from the time that the daily sacrifice shall be taken away, and the abomination that maketh desolate set up, there shall be a thousand two hundred and ninety days. Blessed is he that waiteth, and cometh to the thousand three hundred and five and thirty days"* (Daniel 12:11–12). The Lord will return after 1,260 days. This is calculated from the time the Antichrist sets up the abomination of desolation. He will probably remove this abomination and set up the sanctuary again over a period of 30 days, that is, until the 1,290 days have passed (Daniel 9:24). In the following 45 days, till the 1,335 days are completed, the Jewish people will be purified, as we are told in Zechariah 13:9. These purified Jews will then reign with the Lord as the remnant and have part in the millennial kingdom. This is why Daniel is told, *"Blessed is he that waiteth, and cometh to the thousand three hundred and five and thirty days."*

In this time of the Great Tribulation and the reign of terror of the Antichrist, people will increasingly fall prey to demonic doctrines and will be introduced to occultic practices. Satan himself will seize the power over the world through the Antichrist and demonically deceive this world through signs and lying wonders. This, of course, will not be without results, particularly in Israel (2nd Thessalonians 2:10).

The book of Revelation speaks of the occult deception in the darkest hour of human history: *"And the rest of the men which were not killed by these plagues yet repented not of the works of their hands, that they should not worship devils, and idols of gold, and silver, and brass, and stone, and of wood: which neither can see, nor hear, nor walk"* (Revelation 9:20). This phase of the endtimes will produce many false prophets. Jesus warned of these urgently in His Olivet Discourse: *"And many false prophets shall rise, and shall deceive many"* (Matthew 24:11). *"For there shall arise false Christs, and false prophets, and shall shew great signs and wonders; insomuch that, if it were possible, they shall deceive the very elect"* (Matthew 24:24, compare also to 2nd Peter 2:1). The Antichrist will be the greatest of all false prophets (Revelation 19:20).

After His return, Jesus will destroy all idolatry and all false prophets and with a rod of iron, He will see that nothing like it arises again. At that time, there will be no other religions in this world.

Many expositors are of the opinion that Zechariah 13:5–6 refers to Jesus. However, I believe that false prophets is much more fitting because of the preceding verses. Verse 5 begins with the words, *"But he shall say...,*" following the preceding verse, *"The false prophet will say..."* This prophet states, *"I am no prophet, I am an husbandman."* With Jesus, it was the other way around. He was the True Prophet to whom Moses even referred to, saying, *"The LORD thy God will raise up unto thee a Prophet from the midst of thee, of thy brethren, like unto me; unto him ye shall hearken"* (Deuteronomy 18:15). In contrast to this, Jesus was no husbandman (farmer – NIV), but a carpenter from Nazareth.

Verse 6 begins with the words, *"And one shall say unto him...,"* which refer to the above person, the false prophet. As far as the wounds in his hands are concerned, The Amplified Bible says, *"What are these wounds on your breast – between your hands,"* and these could be scars, or something similar. It was commonplace in those days for idolatrous ceremonies to include self-inflicted wounds in a state of ecstasy. Think of the priests of Baal who wounded themselves with knives in 1st Kings 18:26–29.

The Past Which Points To The Future

Verses 7–9 speak again of the consequences of the rejection of Jesus, which reach beyond that time to the endtimes, even to the millennial kingdom.

"Awake, O sword, against my shepherd, and against the man that is my fellow saith the LORD of hosts: smite the shepherd, and the sheep shall be scattered: and

I will turn mine hand upon the little ones. And it shall come to pass, that in all the land, saith the LORD, two parts therein shall be cut off and die; but the third shall be left therein. And I will bring the third part through the fire, and will refine them as silver is refined, and will try them as gold is tried: they shall call on my name, and I will hear them: I will say, It is my people: and they shall say, The LORD is my God." Jesus is, in contrast to the false prophet (Zechariah 13) and the false shepherd (Zechariah 11), the One whom God calls "My shepherd" and "My fellow."

The sword of God was directed against the Good Shepherd in whom was no sin. God put the guilt of man on His fellow, the Man after His own heart, who did not move from His Father's side during His life on earth, on His beloved Son in whom He had only pleasure. This verse could also be described as the heart of the Gospel. It surpasses our power of imagination, but reveals God's immeasurable love for the sinner, in that He gave the Man who was closest to Him for us.

It is said that the New Testament Gospels quote the prophet Zechariah more than any other prophet in the reports of Jesus' suffering. Thus we find this reference to Zechariah in Matthew 26:31: *"Then saith Jesus unto them, All ye shall be offended because of me this night: for it is written, I will smite the shepherd, and the sheep of the flock shall be scattered abroad."* The disciples dispersed already when Jesus was taken captive; they all forsook Him (John 16:32 and Mark 14:50–52). Practically the entire nation was taken captive by the Romans and dispersed among the nations approximately 30 years later.

The verse continues, *"...and I will turn mine hand upon the little ones"* (Zechariah 13:7). These words refer to those who are poor and weak. At first, it was the disciples whom Jesus gathered around Himself after His resurrection and then gave the task of evangelizing the world. They were all poor and weak. Peter had denied His Lord and wanted to return to his former job as a fisherman. The others were also disappointed and hid behind closed doors for fear of the Jews. But Jesus did not let go of them. He gave them authority and sent them out to build His Church. Many from out of the nations were weak and despised by the Jews, but were added to the Church. The Lord turned His hand upon the nations.

Verses 8–9 do not seem to have been completely fulfilled when the Romans attacked. According to my knowledge, these verses speak of an endtime war, all the more so as they coincide with the refining and salvation of a remnant of the Jews who call upon the Name of the Lord. This shows us that the land of Israel has a terrible time ahead of her with various grave conflicts. Think of the nations surrounding Israel (compare Zechariah 12) or the nations of the North, such as the Assyrians or Gog from the land of Magog, which probably refers to the Islamic nations. Think also of the beast in Daniel 7 which corresponds to the first beast in Revelation 13. This beast is at the head of the Western nations. It unites with the second beast in Revelation 13 which arises out of the earth, that is in the land of Israel (Zechariah 11:16). This second beast corresponds to the Antichrist, the greatest of all false prophets, who, according to my understanding of Scripture, will have his seat in Jerusalem. In the first time of relative "peace and safety" it will be a kind of "security force" for Israel. Later on, it will develop into an occupying power. According to Daniel 11, the king of the North (Syria) and the king of the South (Egypt) and others will fight against the second beast and his protectoral troops in Israel. According to Ezekiel 38 and 39, Gog and his allies will march into a relatively safe land and cover it like a cloud. Finally, the Battle of Armageddon will take place.

Certainly, many wars that are mentioned in the prophetic books are identical. Nonetheless, there will be many attacks on Israel, which will cost many lives and bring them to their knees. Two-thirds of the people will perish in the war described in verse 8, and accordingly, only one-third will remain. Even this last third will be refined to be saved as a remnant. They will call upon the name of the Lord and the Lord will answer them and say, *"It is my people."* They will answer, *"The LORD is my God."*

Why Will Such A Refining Be Necessary?

In the future, there will be a tremendous division among the Jewish people. Many will forsake the faith of the fathers (2nd Peter 3:4) and enter into the covenant with the Antichrist (Daniel 9:27). They will not believe in the return of the Messiah, they will betray their own brothers and they will beat their own fellow men (Matthew 24:10). The love in their hearts will grow cold (Matthew 24:12) because lawlessness will develop to its fullest extent through the *"lawless one"* (2nd Thessalonians 2:7–8). According to Daniel 12:10, many in Israel will be tried and purified, but the wicked will continue to act wickedly. Only the wise will understand. Matthew 24:12 says, *"And because iniquity shall abound, the love of many shall wax cold."* Who is meant by "many"? It cannot mean the world because there is no love in the world, and the Church of Jesus Christ will have already been raptured at the time of the Great Tribulation. So "many" must mean the masses of the Jewish people. Matthew 24 refers to the situation of the Jews directly before Jesus returns.

The expression "many" refers to those mentioned in Daniel 9:27, *"And he shall confirm the covenant with many for one week: and in the midst of the week he shall cause the sacrifice and the oblation to cease, and for the overspreading of abominations he shall make it desolate, even until the consummation,* and that determined shall be poured upon the desolate.* " In Daniel 12:3, "many" are also mentioned: *"And they that be wise shall shine as the brightness of the firmament; and they that turn many to righteousness as the stars for ever and ever.*" In contrast to this, there will also be an apostate Jewry. The following verses confirm this: "*...knowing this first, that there shall come in the last days scoffers, walking after their own lusts, and saying, Where is the promise of his coming? For since the fathers fell asleep, all things continue as they were from the beginning of creation*" (2nd Peter 3:3–4, compare also to Ezekiel 12:21 onwards).

Peter's first and second epistle is addressed to the Jews (1 Peter 1:1 and 2 Peter 3:1). The "fathers" are the patriarchs of Judaism. Because so many have fallen away from the faith, have ignored the law of Moses, and have entered into a covenant with the Antichrist, many will not be able to enter into the Messianic kingdom and will perish (compare also to Ezekiel 20:36–38).

Despite all the positive statements in Zechariah, and God's faithfulness with which He is leading His people to the goal, we may not withhold God's warning. God is holy and He is to be taken seriously. It is not easy to explain this last part of chapter 13 and the first verses of Zechariah 14. I am almost tempted to find another explanation for them, but I cannot.

Zechariah's statements are an earnest warning to all people to let the Good Shepherd convict them. Therein lies the whole idea of the matter; God gave His only Son for us out of love. The sword hit His fellow man. Therefore, those who persist in their rejection of the Lord have no further sacrifice. The book of Revelation says that the people who pledge their allegiance to the Antichrist after the Rapture of the Church and receive his sign have no more chance of being saved (Revelation 14:9–12; 16:2). But the Bible also describes those people those overcome during the Tribulation and do not receive the sign; these people will reign with Christ (Revelation 15:2–3 onwards and 20:4). This all applies also to the Jewish people. Therefore, the Bible says, with great emphasis, *"To day if ye will hear his voice, harden not your hearts"* (Hebrews 3:15).

CHAPTER 19

THE LAST WAR REPORT

"Behold, the day of the LORD cometh, and thy spoil shall be divided in the midst of thee. For I will gather all nations against Jerusalem to battle; and the city shall be taken, and the houses rifled, and the women ravished; and half of the city shall go forth into captivity, and the residue of the people shall not be cut off from the city. Then shall the LORD go forth, and fight against those nations, as when he fought in the day of battle. And his feet shall stand in that day upon the mount of Olives, which is before Jerusalem on the east, and the mount of Olives shall cleave in the midst thereof toward the east and toward the west, and there shall be a very great valley; and half of the mountain shall remove toward the north, and half of it toward the south. And ye shall flee to the valley of the mountains; for the valley of the mountains shall reach unto Azal: yea, ye shall flee, like as ye fled from before the earthquake in the days of Uzziah king of Ju-

dah: and the LORD my God shall come, and all the saints with thee. And it shall come to pass in that day, that the light shall not be clear, nor dark" (Zechariah 14:1–6).

This last war before Christ returns is probably the Battle of Armageddon because it is not between **certain** nations, but **all** nations (verse 2). Zechariah wrote of Christ's visible and triumphant return with His saints to subdue the nations that have been fighting against Israel, and of the immediate establishment of the Messianic kingdom. This event has not yet been fulfilled. It refers to that great day when the Lord will stand upon the Mount of Olives, causing it to split in half. Notice the following terms written in this connection: *"Behold, the day of the LORD cometh"* (verse 1); *"...in the day of battle" (verse 3); and "His feet shall stand in that day..."* (verse 4).

This passage contains a summary of the events written in chapters 12 and 13. These events are referred to again, and their further development is revealed. Although the descriptions are not necessarily chronological, we must put them together like the pieces of a puzzle to get the whole picture. The sequence of events could be as follows:

Jerusalem is attacked by the surrounding nations in Zechariah 12, causing civil war to develop (12:2; 14:14). The attack of the king from the North, behind which stands Gog, from the land of Magog, with his allies, could coincide at that time. It is also quite possible that we are primarily concerned with Islamic lands. Later on, Jerusalem will be attacked by all the nations and will be involved in a terrible war (12:3). Two-thirds of Israel's population will perish in this war (13:8). Jerusalem will be captured and half of the city will be led into captivity (14:3). But then the Lord will arise to fight against the nations, which does not necessarily coincide with His visible return. He will coordinate the events in such a way that the enemies are beaten (14:3). The horses will shy, their riders will be crazed and the nations will be blinded (12:4). This means that the war strategy of which people are so proud of today, and which is demonstrated and marketed by the media, will end in chaos. The Lord will destroy the hostile nations (12:9, 14) through supernatural events (14:12–13). The Mount of Olives will divide for the flight and protection of the Jews (14:4–5). The remainder of Israel and Jerusalem will go through these events, but will call upon the Name of the Lord and will be protected (13:9 and 12:8). The half of Jerusalem that the nations cannot destroy will strengthen themselves in the Lord and defend against their opponents (12:5 and 8). Judah will be saved first because two-thirds of her people will have already perished (12:6–7). Then the Lord will appear visibly to His people (14:5). They will see the One whom they had pierced (12:10) and repent wholeheartedly

(12:10–14). They will receive forgiveness, which will result in their spiritual rebirth. They will receive the Holy Spirit and the Messianic kingdom will be established (13:1–6 and 14:6–21).

Zechariah 14:1–5 almost sounds like a live war report. Yet, after countless wars spanning thousands of years, beginning with Cain and Abel and continuing until this present day, this will be the final war report: *"Behold, the day of the LORD cometh, and thy spoil shall be divided in the midst of thee"* (Zechariah 14:1–4). How impressive are the words, *"Behold, the day of the LORD cometh."* The nations think quite differently. Jerusalem, the burdensome stone, must be removed. As far as the United Nations is concerned, Jerusalem will be the only hindrance to a self-established, humanistic world empire in which the God of Israel will have no room. However, what the nations do not realize is that their day will become the day of the Lord. The day of the nations, when they wanted to erase Jerusalem from the face of the earth, will become the day of the Lord and all the nations will be punished.

It is exciting that all nations will be judged because of Jerusalem. The downfall of the warring nations will not take place just anywhere in the world, but in Jerusalem.

Zechariah 1:10–11 reveals how God observes the nations and their actions in connection with Jerusalem. Verses 14–15 describe the Lord's zeal for

Jerusalem as well as His wrath against Jerusalem's enemies. Chapter 2 explains how God judged the world Empires who touched Jerusalem and Judah, and that God views the Jews and Jerusalem as the *"apple of His eye."* Chapter 3 tells how Satan is rebuked because he turns against God's chosen city. The Lord announces that He will destroy all the nations that have gathered against Jerusalem (12:13). Jerusalem will become a burdensome stone on which the nations will cut themselves (12:3). Chapter 14:12–13 shows how the Lord will judge the nations. Chapter 14:2 explains that the Lord gathers them in Jerusalem for the day of judgment: *"For I will gather all nations against Jerusalem to battle."* The nations believe that they are acting on their own initiative, but the hand of God is behind it to judge them. Now the climax has been reached, and God's intervention on behalf of Zion is imminent. The nations' actions regarding Jerusalem have finally reached their peak; the measure is now full and the nations have become ripe for judgment.

Jerusalem's Weakening

"For I will gather all nations against Jerusalem to battle; and the city shall be taken, and the houses rifled, and the women ravished; and half the city shall go forth into captivity, and the residue of the people shall not be cut off from the city" (Zechariah 14:2).

Initially, the nations will gain a victory over Jerusalem,

which will have terrible results. They will be strengthened in pursuit of their goal, and Israel will become extremely weakened. In view of this situation, you might think the Lord had forgotten His promises to Israel. Where has the Lord's zeal for Jerusalem gone? Where is the fulfillment of His promises for the future? Jerusalem is the city of the Messiah; it is the city of David's descendants, to whom God has promised that there will never be a lack of a descendant on his throne. Is this a lie, or perhaps only a dream? Isn't the Bible true? Or is it just a book like any other? The Jews grieved and swore once by the rivers of Babylon, *"If I forget thee, O Jerusalem..."*. Has God forgotten Jerusalem?

The war report from the "mother" of all wars will be considered "breaking news" at that time. The media will concern themselves primarily with this topic, and all other wars will be of secondary importance. Numerous correspondents and reporters will comment on the situation of the nations and will deliver endless war strategies and Jerusalem's imminent downfall. The media will keep the nations informed down to the final detail. We can almost hear them saying, "The major attack that began a few weeks ago with the gathering of the nation's troops outside Jerusalem is coming to a climax. The city was quickly captured despite its bitter resistance. Chaos has broken out among the inhabitants. People are fleeing; there are a number of dead enemies (traitors to the anti-Christian empire) lying in the streets, including children. After the armed forces began robbing gold from the banks and, as in Kosovo, the women were raped, comparative peace now reigns. A special unit is engaged in transporting thousands of prisoners away. The power of our enemy is broken and the nation's goal has almost been reached. The final solution to the Jewish problem is at hand."

The Great Turning Point

Yet the day, which will become night for Israel, will not end with the nation's victory. Suddenly, the Lord will *"...go forth, and fight against those nations, as when he fought in the day of battle"* (Zechariah 14:3). When the Jews have reached their lowest point, and all further resistance seems so hopeless that they have to surrender themselves before their enemies, and above all before God, a turning point will take place in their favor. One report will follow another, as was the case in the days following the World Trade Center attack and collapse. Suddenly, losses in their own ranks will be noticed. A mysterious illness will strike the soldiers (14:12). Officers of the individual nations will disagree and work against each other. The situation will seem out of control. The military strategy will no longer work, weapons will fail, soldiers will kill one another and racial conflicts will arise. Inexplicable and surprising events will cause great confusion and the general staff will become perplexed (14:13).

Suddenly, a great earthquake will take place: *"And his feet shall stand in that day upon the mount of Olives, which is before Jerusalem on the east, and the mount of Olives shall cleave in the midst thereof toward the east and toward the west, and there shall be a very great valley; and half of the mountain shall remove toward the north, and half of it toward the south"* (Zechariah 14:4). This fulfills of the angel's promise to the disciples the day Jesus ascended into heaven: *"Ye men of Galilee, why stand ye gazing up into heaven? this same Jesus, which is taken up from you into heaven, shall so come in like manner as ye have seen him go into heaven"* (Acts 1:11).

This very event will probably trigger off the earthquake, just as Jesus' death did (Matthew 27:51). His resurrection was accompanied by an earthquake, and His return will also generate one. It could be that the earthquake described in Revelation 16:17–21 coincides with the Battle of Armageddon: *"And he gathered them together into a place called in the Hebrew tongue Armageddon. And the seventh angel poured out his vial into the air; and there came a great voice out of the temple of heaven, from the throne, saying, It is done. And there were voices, and thunders, and lightnings; and there was a great earthquake, such as was not since men were upon the earth, so mighty an earthquake, and so great. And the great city was di-*

vided into three parts, and the cities of the nations fell: and great Babylon came in remembrance before God, to give unto her the cup of the wine of the fierceness of his wrath. And every island fled away, and the mountains were not found. And there fell upon men a great hail out of heaven, every stone about the weight of a talent: and men blasphemed God because of the plague of the hail; for the plague thereof was exceeding great" (Revelation 16:16–21). The Mount of Olives will split in two as a result of the earthquake. For a large number of Jews, the newly erected canyon will open the way of escape: *"And ye shall flee to the valley of the mountains; for the valley of the mountains shall reach unto Azal: yea, ye shall flee, like as ye fled from before the earthquake in the days of Uzziah king of Judah"* (Zechariah 14:5, also compare to Amos 1:1).

Many of the troops that have been hostile toward Israel will be exterminated through these events and a large part of their weapons will be destroyed. There will be a great distress on account of sickness. In addition, the Jews will suddenly find new courage and many will start to believe in God again and will become stronger in the battle against their enemies.

Media correspondents will be almost out of their minds. A few days earlier, everything looked so different. And now? It seems like the story of David and Goliath: Israel (little David) begins to have victory over the great Goliath (the nations). At that time, it was not David who hit Goliath; it was God who guided the stone to hit Goliath right in the forehead. Israel will remember God's intervention in the past and say to one another, "Do you remember the Exodus from Egypt? At that time our fathers were also in an impossible situation. They stood before the Red Sea and Pharaoh pursued them with his troops from behind. Our people were terribly afraid and thought their doom was sealed. Yet Moses said, *'Fear ye not, stand still, and see the salvation of the LORD, which he will shew to you to day: for the Egyptians whom ye have seen to day, ye shall see them again no more for ever. The LORD shall fight for you, and ye shall hold your peace'* (Exodus 14:13–14). Then suddenly, the sea divided and Israel was able to pass through. However, the Egyptians pursuing them drowned in the sea. Therefore, let us be strong in the Lord and call upon His Name. Let's believe in His help, because His promises have not been made void; they will be fulfilled."

The Lord's Visible Return

Zechariah 14:5 reads: "*...and the LORD my God shall come, and all the saints with thee.*" Isaiah 31:4 is the parallel verse: "*For thus hath the LORD spoken unto me, Like as the lion and the young lion roaring on his prey, when a multitude of shepherds is called forth against him, he will not be afraid of their voice,* *nor abase himself for the noise of them: so shall the LORD of hosts come down to fight for mount Zion, and for the hill thereof.*" At this return of the God of Israel, the Jewish population will be shaken to the core and will repent. Why? Because they'll have experienced the God of Abraham, Isaac and Jacob. Their faith in Him will be strengthened so that they will have even called upon His Name. But one thing these people have not yet really understood is who this God is. Now they will be able to see that Jesus Christ is the true God of Israel. He will reveal Himself to them (12:10) just as Joseph revealed himself to his brothers after they had rejected him, and then sought help from him years later without knowing who he was.

Israel will then confess, "It is the one we had nailed to the Cross, the One whom we pierced. He was in our midst once before, but we did not want Him." But something else will have a permanent effect; namely, that the Lord will return with His saints. I believe that besides the angels (Matthew 24:31), the Church, which has already been raptured, will be with Him. Consider these passages:

- "*And to you who are troubled rest with us, when the Lord Jesus shall be revealed from heaven with his mighty angels, In flaming fire taking vengeance on them that know not God, and that obey not the gospel of our Lord Jesus Christ: Who shall be punished with everlasting destruction from the presence of the Lord, and from the glory of his power; When he shall come to be glorified in his saints, and to be admired in all them that believe (because our testimony among you was believed) in that day"* (2nd Thessalonians 1:7–10).

- *"And Enoch also, the seventh from Adam, prophesied of these, saying, Behold, the Lord cometh with ten thousands of his saints"* (Jude 1:14).

- *"...at the coming of our Lord Jesus Christ with all his saints"* (1st Thessalonians 3:13).

- *"And I* (John) *saw heaven opened, and behold a white horse; and he that sat upon him was called Faithful and True, and in righteousness he doth judge and make war...And the armies which were in heaven followed him upon white horses, clothed in fine linen, white and clean"* (Revelation 19:11, 14).

Won't it be a great surprise for Israel that, in the meantime, the Lord has chosen a Church out of the nations, with which He will now return? Not only will Israel see Him return (Matthew 24:30), but so will all the other nations and tribes of the earth (Revelation 1:7).

The Lord's return will be accompanied by tremendous supernatural occurrences. An earthquake will cause the division of the Mount of Olives and also in the heavens certain shocking things will take place: *"And it shall come to pass in that day, that the light shall not be clear, nor dark"* (Zechariah 14:6). In many parallel verses, the Bible says that there will be signs in the sun, moon and stars, which will proclaim Christ's imminent return (compare to Mark 13:24–26, Isaiah 13:10 and 34:4, Joel 3:4, Amos 5:18, 20 and Revelation 6:12–17).

Thus the Lord will take the ultimate war report into His hands. The people will not need to watch television, listen to the radio or read the newspaper; they will all experience it live and will gaze toward heaven when the light of His return arises!

CHAPTER 20

THE MIRACLE OF A NEW DISPENSATION

"But it shall be one day which shall be known to the LORD, not day, nor night: but it shall come to pass, that at evening time it shall be light. And it shall be in that day, that living waters shall go out from Jerusalem; half of them toward the former sea, and half of them toward the hinder sea: in summer and in winter shall it be. And the LORD shall be king over all the earth: in that day shall there be one LORD, and his name one. All the land shall be turned as a plain from Geba to Rimmon south of Jerusalem: and it shall be lifted up, and inhabited in her place, from Benjamin's gate unto the place of the first gate, unto the corner gate, and from the tower of Hananeel unto the king's winepresses. And men shall dwell in it, and there shall be no more utter destruction; but Jerusalem shall be safely inhabited. And this shall be the plague wherewith the LORD will smite all the people that

have fought against Jerusalem; Their flesh shall con-
sume away while they stand upon their feet, and their
eyes shall consume away in their holes, and their
tongue shall consume away in their mouth. And it
shall come to pass in that day, that a great tumult from
the LORD shall be among them; and they shall lay
hold every one on the hand of his neighbour, and his
hand shall rise up against the hand of his neighbour.
And Judah also shall fight at Jerusalem; and the
wealth of all the heathen round about shall be gath-
ered together, gold, and silver, and apparel, in great
abundance. And so shall be the plague of the horse, of
the mule, of the camel, and of the ass, and of all the
beasts that shall be in these tents, as this plague. And
it shall come to pass, that every one that is left of all
the nations which came against Jerusalem shall even
go up from year to year to worship the King, the
LORD of hosts, and to keep the feast of tabernacles.
And it shall be, that whoso will not come up of all the
families of the earth unto Jerusalem to worship the
King, the LORD of hosts, even upon them shall be no
rain. And if the family of Egypt go not up, and come
not, that have no rain; there shall be the plague,
wherewith the LORD will smite the heathen that
come not up to keep the feast of tabernacles. This shall
be the punishment of Egypt, and the punishment of all
nations that come not up to keep the feast of taber-
nacles. In that day shall there be upon the bells of the

horses, HOLINESS UNTO THE LORD; and the pots in the LORD's house shall be like the bowls before the altar. Yea, every pot in Jerusalem and in Judah shall be holiness unto the LORD of hosts: and all they that sacrifice shall come and take of them, and seethe therein: and in that day there shall be no more the Canaanite in the house of the LORD of hosts" (Zechariah 14:7–21).

The preceding chapter took us up to mankind's last war and Jesus' subsequent return: *"And the LORD my God shall come, and all the saints with thee"* (Zechariah 14:5). Now the world has come to rest; the Lord has removed the abomination of desolation (Daniel 9:24 and 12:11–12). Together with its leaders, the anti-Christian world system will have been destroyed (Daniel 9:17; 2nd Thessalonians 2:8 and Revelation 18:19–20). The dead who had believed on Jesus and did not receive the mark of the beast in the Great Tribulation will be raised, as will the dead saints of the Old Testament (Revelation 20:4 and Daniel 12:1–3). The entire land will be purified (Zechariah 13:2–6). The last judgment on the Israelites will have taken place (Ezekiel 20:35–39 and Matthew 25:1–13), as will the last judgment upon the nations. Subsequently, those who may enter into the Messianic kingdom will be revealed (Matthew 25:31–46). The most Holy (*"most holy place"*– NIV) will be reestablished (Daniel 9:24), in that the Temple written of in Ezekiel

40–47 will be rebuilt. Swords will be turned into plowshares (Isaiah 2:4) and a new age will have dawned: The age of the Messianic kingdom.

What will be the miracles of this new age?

A New Day Dawns

"And it shall come to pass in that day, that the light shall not be clear, nor dark: But it shall be one day which shall be known to the LORD, not day, nor night: but it shall come to pass that at evening time it shall be light" (Zechariah 14:6–7). As a proclamation of the Lord's imminent return, the heavenly bodies will withhold their light (Matthew 24:29 and Revelation 6:12–14). Then the sign of the Son of man will appear in the heavens and Jesus will return in glory (Matthew 24:30). There will probably be a new kind of creation, similar to that described in Genesis. Darkness had accompanied the divine judgments described by Zechariah; the removal of sin was accomplished. Everything lay beneath a gray mist, *"...neither day nor night,"* but now the darkness will have given way to the light.

The millennium of peace under Jesus' rule will be inaugurated after all the preparations have been made. This particular day, known only by the Lord, will be the first of a new age (Revelation 20:4). Darkness will disappear and the glory of the Lord will open up like the door to a glorious garden. His light will end the evening of the Great Tribulation, *"At evening time it shall be light,"* and will usher in a new day. The "new day" of the millennium of peace will be characterized by the glory of Jesus. This light will probably shine throughout the entire Messianic age and will flood the ends of the earth.

The establishment of the "new dispensation" will create completely different conditions for life. The climate and topography will be changed, and nature will be transformed. People will live much longer and peace will reign in the animal kingdom. Evil will be banned and the righteousness of the Lord will reign. The sun will no longer set, but will shine seven times brighter. The moon will no longer wane. Trees will bear fruit every month and will contribute to the continual health of the nations (Isaiah 11:1–10, 30:26, 35:1–14, 60:1–4 and 19–22 and 65:18–25, Ezekiel 47:12, Romans 8:21–25, Revelation 20:1–3, 21 and 22:2). We can conclude from this that God's ways for all who believe on Him never end in darkness, but in His bright light!

A Stream Of Living Water

"And it shall be in that day, that living waters shall go out from Jerusalem; half of them toward the former sea, and half of them toward the hinder sea: in summer and in winter shall it be" (Zechariah 14:8). Ezekiel foresaw this river and saw it flow from under the threshold of the Temple. Its source was like a foun-

tain (Zechariah 13:1), but then it became deeper and even more powerful. First, the water reached Ezekiel's ankles, but became so deep that he could not wade through it. This water that went forth from Jerusalem reached the eastern coast of the Dead Sea and made everything come alive, so that the land became fertile again and the salt water was full of fish (Ezekiel 47:1–12).

However, Zechariah tells us that these living waters also reach the Mediterranean and do not cease to flow in summer or winter. Israel will never again lack water. This river that proceeds from the Lord and His Temple will create a paradise on earth. Israel and all the other nations will profit from this constantly flowing river. It points to the river at the end of the biblical Revelation, which proceeds from the throne of God (Revelation 22:1), and to the heavenly goal of God with all people who have given their lives to Jesus.

Spiritually, this stream of living water makes it clear to us that the abundant fullness of life is to be found only in God. Jesus said to the Samaritan woman, *"But whosoever drinketh of the water that I shall give him shall never thirst: but the water that I shall give him shall be in him a well of water springing up into everlasting life"* (John 4:14). According to Scripture, the Lord promised those who believe on Him that streams of living water will flow from them (John 7:38–39).

The Lord Will Be King

"And the LORD shall be king over all the earth: in that day shall there be one LORD, and his name one" (Zechariah 14:9). The day is coming during which all religious books will be thrown away and there will be no more founders of religions. The day is coming when no theory, philosophy or ideology will be valid and all idols will be forgotten. This is the day when all people will recognize that there is only one King and only one Name above all names: Jesus Christ, the Messiah of Israel.

The Bible describes Jesus as the King of kings and Lord of lords. He has a Name which is above all names, and there is no other Name under the heavens whereby we can be saved. Before Jesus Christ, every knee will bow and every tongue will have to confess that He is Lord (compare to Revelation 1:5; 1 Timothy 6:15; Acts 4:12; Philippians 2:9–11 and Zechariah 14:16–17). However, He will be King not only of Israel, but of the whole earth. Jerusalem is His city of residence and from there He will rule over all nations (Zechariah 2:14–15). Jerusalem will be exalted and become the capital of the world. Psalm 97:1 says: *"The LORD reigneth; let the earth rejoice; let the multitude of isles be glad thereof."* The book of Revelation explains it even more clearly: *"And the seventh angel sounded; and there were great voices in heaven, saying, The kingdoms of this world are become the kingdoms of our Lord, and of his Christ; and he shall reign for ever and ever"* (Revelation 11:15).

Topographic Changes

"All the land shall be turned as a plain from Geba to Rimmon south of Jerusalem; and it shall be lifted up, and inhabited in her place, from Benjamin's gate unto the place of the first gate, unto the corner gate, and from the tower of Hananeel unto the king's wine-presses, And men shall dwell in it, and there shall be no more utter destruction; but Jerusalem shall be safely inhabited" (Zechariah 14:10–11). We have already stated that the land of Israel will be changed. One Bible commentary says:

"The whole land of Judah, from Geba in the north (Joshua 21:17) to Rimmon (Joshua 15:32) — probably the southern border, 50 kilometers south-west of Jerusalem — will be transformed into a wide valley, similar to Araba, the low plain which extends from Mount Hermon to the Jordan Valley and to the Dead Sea on the Gulf of Aqaba. Therewith, Jerusalem, whose situation remains unaltered, as the capital of the great King, will lie higher."

Isaiah also referred to this when he said, *"And it shall come to pass in the last days, that the mountain of the LORD's house shall be established in the top of the mountains, and shall be exalted above the hills; and all nations shall flow unto it"* (Isaiah 2:2), and

"The voice of him that crieth in the wilderness, Prepare ye the way of the LORD, make straight in the desert a highway for our God. Every valley shall be exalted, and every mountain and hill shall be made low; and the crooked shall be made straight, and the rough places plain: And the glory of the LORD shall be revealed, and all flesh shall see it together: for the mouth of the LORD hath spoken it" (Isaiah 40:3–5). John the Baptist also proclaimed this message later on. The topographic changes had not taken place at Jesus' First Advent; therefore, this refers to His return.

The land will also be changed spiritually. What we saw in Zechariah 13:1–6 is also described here: Every curse will be removed from Jerusalem (compare to Zechariah 14:21) and Jerusalem will dwell in safety. At that time there will be neither terrorist attacks nor war against Jerusalem, because the Lord Himself will be a fiery wall around Jerusalem and will dwell in her midst (Zechariah 2:9).

Verses 12–15 seem to be a repetition, or a review, of Jerusalem's attack, and of how the Lord will execute judgment at His return (12–14:6).

The Blessing For All Nations

"And it shall come to pass, that every one that is left of all the nations which came against Jerusalem shall even go up from year to year to worship the King, the LORD of hosts, and to keep the feast of

tabernacles. And it shall be, that whoso will not come up of all the families of the earth unto Jerusalem to worship the King, the LORD of hosts, even upon them shall be no rain. And if the family of Egypt go not up, and come not, that have no rain; there shall be the plague, wherewith the LORD will smite the heathen that come not up to keep the feast of tabernacles. This shall be the punishment of Egypt, and the punishment of all nations that come not up to keep the feast of tabernacles. In that day shall there be upon the bells of the horses, HOLINESS UNTO THE LORD; and the pots in the LORD's house shall be like the bowls before the altar. Yea, every pot in Jerusalem and in Judah shall be holiness unto the LORD of hosts: and all they that sacrifice shall come and take of them, and seethe therein: and in that day there shall be no more the Canaanite in the house of the LORD of hosts" (Zechariah 14:16–21). All nations will be included in Israel's blessing and the blessing of the kingdom of Christ. Here, that which God promised Abraham thousands of years ago will be completely fulfilled: *"...in thee shall all families of the earth be blessed"* (Genesis 12:3).

The Feast of Tabernacles (also known as Succoth), in which the nations are to participate, plays a very important role because it had always been a prophetic feast which included the nations. On one hand, Israel was to remember the time she wandered in the wilderness. After leaving Egypt, Succoth was the first place they came, *"And the children of Israel journeyed from Rameses to Succoth"* (Exodus 12:37). The feast was to be celebrated for seven days every year in memory of the fact that they had lived in very simple booths in the wilderness (Leviticus 23.42–43). The roofs of the booths gave the Israelites very little protection, so they could see the pillar of cloud or of fire through the branches. At Succoth, this cloud of the glory of God appeared anew and led the people (Exodus 40:38).

At the Feast of Tabernacles, the Israelites were also to remember that the Lord in His glory watches over and guides His people. Israel was simultaneously under *"...the shadow of the Almighty"* (Psalm 91:1–2). The Feast of Tabernacles, therefore, was a joyful feast: *"...and ye shall rejoice before the LORD your God seven days"* (Leviticus 23:40 and Deuteronomy 16:14–15).

On the other hand, the Feast of Tabernacles points to the millennium of peace under the rule of the Messiah, in which His divine glory will dwell in the Temple at Jerusalem again: *"And the LORD will create upon every dwelling place of mount Zion, and upon her assemblies, a cloud and smoke by day, and the shining of a flaming fire by night: for upon all the glory shall be a defence. And there shall be a tabernacle for a shadow in the daytime from the heat, and for a place of refuge, and for a covert from storm and from rain"* (Isaiah 4:5–6). The nations will also take part in this millennium of peace. Amos prophesied, *"In that day will I raise up the tabernacle of David that is fallen, and close up the breaches thereof; and I will raise up his ruins, and I will build it as in the days of old: That they may possess the remnant of Edom, and of all the heathen, which are called by my name, saith the LORD that doeth this"* (Amos 9:11–12). James, the pastor of the first church at Jerusalem, quoted these words to the young church which was called to salvation through the Gospel (Acts 15:16–17). The fallen-down tabernacle of David (Succoth) will be rebuilt (Israel's endtime restoration), and the nations will also come under the blessing of the glory of God.

In this connection, it is interesting to note that the Jews had to sacrifice 70 bullocks during the seven-day Feast of Tabernacles (Numbers 29:12–34). Why 70? Because the list of nations in Genesis 10 comprises exactly 70 nations. All the nations are to be included in the salvation of Israel through the sacrifice of the greatest Jew, Jesus Christ. *"And in his name shall the Gentiles trust"* (Matthew 12:21).

But we also see a certain severity in the kingdom of Christ. It is by no means a kingdom in which everything is tolerated and in which everyone can do as he or she pleases. The Lord will rule the nations in righteousness and holiness with His strong arm (Revelation

12:5): Sin will not be tolerated, but will be judged immediately (Isaiah 65:20). All the more so because Satan, the deceiver of mankind, will be bound during
this time (Revelation 20:1–3). Thus the nations will
not merely be invited to the Feast of Tabernacles, but
they will be commanded to take part in it and in do
ing so, honor and worship the King.

It is striking that Egypt is given a special mention.
This is perhaps because she, in particular, oppressed
the Jewish people in their beginnings. Yet Isaiah also
promises Egypt that she will be converted in the endtimes: *"And the LORD shall smite Egypt: he shall
smite and heal it: and they shall return even to the
LORD, and he shall be intreated of them, and shall
heal them. In that day shall there be a highway out of
Egypt to Assyria, and the Assyrian shall come into
Egypt, and the Egyptian into Assyria, and the Egyptians shall serve with the Assyrians"* (Isaiah
19:22–23). Why does Isaiah give Egypt's conversion
a special mention? Perhaps because she took Jesus in
when He had to flee from Herod. In any case, God's
absolute justice is revealed in both Isaiah and
Zechariah.

At that time, the holiness of the Lord will fill everything in Israel; even the bells on the horses, the cook-
ing pots and bowls before the altar will be sanctified
(verse 20). Sanctification will include the entirety of
practical life.

The book of Zechariah ends with these words: *"...and in that day there shall be no more the Canaanite in the house of the LORD of hosts"* (verse 20). The NIV renders the word "Canaanite" as "merchant." Merchants were symbolic for cheating, cunning and deception in those days. *"He is a merchant, the balances of deceit are in his hand: he loveth to oppress"* (Hosea 12:7). Where sanctification (setting apart) reigns, there can be no more contamination through sin! The events Zechariah describes mainly focus on the future of Israel and the nations. According to my understanding of Scripture, the Rapture of the Church will take place before the worst time of the Great Tribulation. When we read chapters 12–14, and notice how the endtimes are already beginning and their contours are becoming clearer on the horizon of world history, shouldn't we live more sanctified and devoted lives to Christ, as we wait for Him and His return for the Church? *"Wherefore, beloved, seeing that ye look for such things, be diligent that ye may be found of him in peace, without spot, and blameless"* (2nd Peter 3:14).

౪

⮕ *Tap into the Bible analysis of top prophecy authorities...*

Midnight Call is a hard-hitting Bible-based magazine loaded with news, commentary, special features, and teaching, illustrated with explosive color pictures and graphics. Join hundreds of thousands of readers in 140 countries who enjoy this magazine regularly!

⮕ *The world's leading prophetic Bible magazine*

⮕ *Covering international topics with detailed commentary*

⮕ *Bold, uncompromising biblical stands on issues*

⮕ *Pro-Bible, Pro-family, Pro-life*

12 issues/1 yr. $28.95
24 issues/2 yr. $45

Mail with payment to: Midnight Call • P.O. Box 280008 • Columbia, SC 29228 1052

❏ YES! I would like to subscribe to *Midnight Call* magazine!
    ❏ 12 issues/1 yr. $28⁹⁵ ❏ 24 issues/2 yr. $45
    ❏ Cash ❏ Check ❏ Master/Visa/Discover
With Credit Card, you may also dial toll-free, 1–800–845–2420

Card# _____ Exp: _____

Name: _____

Address: _____

City: _____ St: _____ Zip: _____